2008
THE BEST 10-MINUTE PLAYS
FOR TWO ACTORS

SMITH AND KRAUS PUBLISHERS
Short Plays and 10-Minute Plays Collections

Christopher Durang Vol. I: 27 Short Plays

Frank D. Gilroy Vol. II: 15 One-Act Plays

Israel Horovitz Vol. I: 16 Short Plays

Romulus Linney 17 Short Plays

Terrence McNally Vol. I: 15 Short Plays

Lanford Wilson: 21 Short Plays

Act One Festival 1995: The Complete One-Act Plays

Act One Festival 1994: The Complete One-Act Plays

EST Marathon 1999: The Complete One-Act Plays

EST Marathon 1998: The Complete One-Act Plays

EST Marathon 1997: The Complete One-Act Plays

EST Marathon 1996: The Complete One-Act Plays

EST Marathon 1995: The Complete One-Act Plays

EST Marathon 1994: The Complete One-Act Plays

Twenty One-Acts from 20 Years at the Humana Festival 1975–1995

Women's Project and Productions Rowing to America & Sixteen Other Short Plays

8 TENS @ 8 Festival: 30 10-Minute Plays from the Santa Cruz Festivals I–VI

30 Ten-Minute Plays from the Actors Theatre of Louisville for 2 Actors

30 Ten-Minute Plays from the Actors Theatre of Louisville for 3 Actors

30 Ten-Minute Plays from the Actors Theatre of Louisville for 4, 5, and 6 Actors

2004: The Best 10-Minute Plays for Two Actors

2004: The Best 10-Minute Plays for Three or More Actors

2005: The Best 10-Minute Plays for Two Actors

2005: The Best 10-Minute Plays for Three or More Actors

2006: The Best 10-Minute Plays for Two Actors

2006: The Best 10-Minute Plays for Three or More Actors

2007: The Best 10-Minute Plays for Two Actors

2007: The Best 10-Minute Plays for Three or More Actors

2008: The Best 10-Minute Plays for Two Actors

2008: The Best 10-Minute Plays for Three or More Actors

To receive prepublication information about upcoming Smith and Kraus books and information about special promotions, send us your e-mail address at info@smithandkraus.com with a subject line of MAILING LIST. You may receive our annual catalogue, free of charge, by sending your name and address to catalogue@smithandkraus.com. Call toll-free to order (888) 282-2881 or visit us at SmithandKraus.com.

2008

THE BEST 10-MINUTE PLAYS
FOR TWO ACTORS

Edited by Lawrence Harbison

CONTEMPORARY PLAYWRIGHT SERIES

A Smith and Kraus Book
Hanover, New Hampshire

Published by Smith and Kraus, Inc.
177 Lyme Road, Hanover, NH 03755
www.SmithandKraus.com / (888) 282-2881

First Edition: April 2009
10 9 8 7 6 5 4 3 2 1

Manufactured in the United States of America
Cover and text design by Julia Hill Gignoux, Freedom Hill Design
Production editing and formatting by Electric Dragon Productions
Cover photo by Carlo Damocles; Antwan Ward and Melanie Nicholls-King
in Linda Faigao-Hall's *The A-Word*

ISBN-13 978-1-57525-709-9 / ISBN-10 1-57525-709-2
Library of Congress Control Number: 2009923521

Contents

Plays for Two Men

Plays for Two Women

Foreword

What makes a good ten-minute play? Well, for one thing the characters have to be interesting and the story compelling. Most importantly, though, the play has to have a beginning, a middle, and an end. It has to be a complete play. Many of the ten-minute plays I have read have interesting characters embedded in a good story; but they come off as scenes rather than plays. Perhaps, some of them are.

I think all of the plays in this volume have interesting characters and stories. Here, you will find fine new plays by established playwrights such as Joan Ackermann, Frederick Stroppel, Don Nigro, Laura Harrington, Jack Neary, Neena Beber, Julian Sheppard, and Wendy MacLeod, as well as equally good plays by newcomers such as Caitlin Montanye Parrish, Brian Dykstra, John Shanahan, Ron Fitzgerald, Bruce Shearer, Francine Volpe, Stephanie Allison Walker, Bekah Brunstetter, Ian August, and Linda Faigao-Hall.

I hope you enjoy reading these plays; but more important, I hope you produce them.

Lawrence Harbison
Brooklyn, New York

PLAYS FOR
ONE MAN
AND
ONE WOMAN

Apricot Sunday

ED CARDONA, JR.

Produced by La Ley Theatre at the Alma Schapiro Center for
Music and Theater, Columbia University, New York City,
April 11, 2005. Directed by Javierantonio González.
Cast: Maria—Kelly Eubanks; Nelson—Kyle Knauf.

CHARACTERS

MARIA, thirty-three, corporate type.

NELSON, twenty-eight, blue-collar type.

SETTING

A seedy motel room.

TIME

The present: late evening.

• • •

Nelson stands upstage center leaning against the wall. He is dressed in a pair of boxers and one black sock. The bed, at center stage left, is messy and covered with apricots and clothing. Its headboard is flush against the stage left wall. A night stand, downstage left, sits by the bed. A dim lamp, a flashing clock radio, and a small Bible are on the night stand. A TV sits on a bureau pressed against the stage right wall. An I Love Lucy *episode plays with its volume turned down. A boom box sits on a chair in the corner of the room, upstage right. A door, upstage left, leads into the bathroom, offstage. Sinatra's "My Way" plays softly from the radio. The song should play continuously through the entire performance. Lights fade up.*

MARIA: *(Offstage. From hotel bathroom.)* You are useless! Absolutely useless! Be a man! You PUSSY!

(Nelson does not respond, and shows no reaction.)

MARIA: *(Offstage.)* GO!

NELSON: Do you want me to sing?

MARIA: Whatever! Just go, you useless—

NELSON: *(A capella.)* "WHY IS IT NOW? That soon without you; I will no longer laugh or smile. My friend, I know you well, but not well enough to know, why I must—"

MARIA: *(Offstage.)* Hey stallion!

NELSON: You don't have to call me that anymore.

MARIA: *(Offstage.)* What did you say, king of my pussy?

NELSON: *(Angry.)* . . . You don't have to call me by those names anymore!

MARIA: *(Offstage.)* I can't hear you, mountaineer of my tits!

NELSON: I said—

MARIA: *(Offstage.)* I'll be right out!

NELSON: (A capella.) "Regrets, my life is full; but then again, God is what gave birth to me, so I do what I must, and always see it through, with out exemption, because that is what a man must do."

(Maria enters. She is dressed in a man's dress shirt. Her lipstick is smeared and her hair is a mess. She waltzes around the room.)

MARIA: (A capella.) ". . . Yes, I've bit off more than I could chew. But I faced it all, and stood tall, and I'm doing it my way." (Beat.) What did you say, honey?

NELSON: I said . . . you don't have to call me those names anymore.

MARIA: I thought you liked to hear them.

NELSON: Only when I'm fucking you . . . do you understand?

MARIA: Yes. But this time I'm on top.

NELSON: Take my shirt off.

MARIA: OK.

NELSON: Did you bring the Lucy Ricardo dress?

MARIA: I'm not sure. I'll check.

(Maria exits into the bathroom.)

NELSON: (Toward bathroom door.) That's the only way you're getting on top.

MARIA: (Offstage.) I'm looking!

(Nelson eats an apricot and picks up the other black sock and stretches it out.)

NELSON: For every year that goes by. I get . . . just a little bit more castrated!

(Maria enters dressed in a bra, underwear, and an apron; she waltzes around the room.)

MARIA: . . . You really think so?

NELSON: Yes.

MARIA: Men rule the world.

NELSON: Not the right ones.

MARIA: I left the dress, but I brought this cute apron . . . same thing.

NELSON: I guess.

MARIA: (A capella.) "I faced what I could and played all the roles that I should, with pink dresses, bobby pins, business suits, and motherly caresses when they were due."

(Nelson places a couple of apricots into the sock he is holding.)

NELSON: Sit down.

(Maria waltzes around the room.)

MARIA: (A capella.) "I've loved, compromised, and cried. I've filled my share of pies. But tonight there will be no real tears to wipe aside . . . Though I do find it very not amusing."

NELSON: Come over here.

MARIA: What?

NELSON: Come here.

MARIA: Meet me halfway.

NELSON: OK.

(They cross to each other.)

NELSON: You're beautiful.

(She grabs his crotch.)

MARIA: . . . I can assure you, you're not castrated.

NELSON: With all of the feminists, gays, Mr. Moms, and fag TV, I'm a dying breed. For what's a man got, if his nuts are no longer worshipped?

MARIA: Should we check on the kids?

NELSON: I told you that we don't have to do that anymore. Let's just worry about us, being us.

MARIA: I liked that part . . . I would have made a great mother.

NELSON: I'm sure you would have. Can we get back to business?

(Nelson picks up an apricot.)

MARIA: OK, but I think we're out of condoms.

NELSON: Do you know that apricots were used in the nectar of Greek and Roman gods?

MARIA: (Uninterested.) . . . Really?

NELSON: The Persians called them the eggs of the sun.

MARIA: Well, I've got the eggs from God. How about paying some lip service to those—

NELSON: Apricot pits are also used in cosmetics.

(Nelson bites into the apricot exposing the juicy pulp. He smears the juice all over Maria's face.)

MARIA: We need a condom.

NELSON: This is exactly what I'm talking about. I haven't felt the insides of a woman in years. Nothing but plastic. I might as well be a dildo.

MARIA: You know the pill makes my hair fall out.

NELSON: It's not like I'm a stranger—

MARIA: There is a vending machine in the bathroom.

NELSON: No . . . this time I'm not using one.

(Nelson throws Maria on the bed and rips the apron off.)

MARIA: Asshole, get off—

(Maria slaps Nelson and then grabs and hangs onto his balls.)

NELSON: Ah . . . easy.

MARIA: Get one from the bathroom. And that's all I want to hear about that.

NELSON: OK . . . But—

(Maria slaps Nelson across the face. Nelson exits into the bathroom, beat, he re-enters, finds his pants, and searches the pockets for money. He's broke.)

NELSON: Can I have some money?

(Maria picks up her purse and pulls out a few dollars.)

NELSON: I always give you every cent I have.

MARIA: Did I say anything?

(Nelson exits into the bathroom.)

MARIA: *(To herself.)* Which isn't much.

(Maria lies in bed and begins to toss an apricot into the air. Nelson is heard offstage fighting with the condom machine, cursing. Maria bites an apricot in half and places the two pieces over her eyes. She lies in bed motionless. Nelson enters.)

NELSON: The machine is out of condoms.

MARIA: *(Motionless.)* You sure?

NELSON: Yes.

MARIA: Try the front desk.

NELSON: The machine ate my money.

MARIA: *(Boisterous laugh.)* Haaaaa-haaaaa!

NELSON: *(Sarcastically.)* Oh, that's funny to you?

(Nelson snatches Maria by the hair and begins to drag her into the bathroom.)

NELSON: Oh, how funny is this! Ha, ha, ha, ha!

(They exit into the bathroom. Beat.)

MARIA: *(Offstage. Frantic, but aroused.)* I'm sorry!

NELSON: *(Offstage.)* You try! Let's see you get some fucking condoms out of that fucking machine!

MARIA: *(Offstage.)* Let go of my hair! You're hurting me!

(We hear as Nelson slams Maria into the door.)

MARIA: *(Offstage.)* Not so fucking hard, asshole!

(Maria grabs Nelson by the nuts.)

NELSON: *(Offstage.)* Oow—Oow . . . sorry! Let go . . . LET GO!

MARIA: *(Offstage.)* Who's your Mami?

NELSON: *(Offstage.)* You are!

MARIA: *(Offstage.)* You are so pathetic . . . *(Laughter.)* . . . !

NELSON: I've told you not to laugh at me!

MARIA: *(Offstage.)* PA-THE-TIC!

NELSON: *(Offstage.)* Don't you fucking move!

MARIA: *(Offstage.)* OK!

(Nelson enters and grabs the apricot-filled sock and wraps the open end firmly around his hand. Maria is heard offstage masturbating.)

MARIA: Aaaaaa—aaaaaa—who needs you!

(Nelson stretches the sock out. He exits into the bathroom. He strikes Maria with the sock.)

MARIA: Oow—Ahhhhhh . . . *(Crying.)*

(Beat, Nelson enters.)

NELSON: *(Out of breath.)* . . . How funny did those apricots feel!

MARIA: *(Offstage. Sobbing.)* . . . Ooooooooooooow!

NELSON: *(A capella.)* "I've loved, I've compromised and lied. I've changed my share of diapers and used her insurance. So there will be no tears to wipe aside . . . Though I do find it very not amusing."

MARIA: *(Offstage. Sobbing.)* . . . Honey! Did you pull the handle on the machine?

NELSON: No. I pushed the button.

MARIA: That's not a button, you have to pull the lever!

(Nelson bites into an apricot and listens to the music for a couple of beats. Maria enters still in tears and holding her side with one hand. In the other hand she holds a condom. She sits next to Nelson.)

NELSON: Did you know that apricots can help fight cancer? That they are pretty much the cure for cancer, but big biz and the government keeps it from us?

MARIA: Only because you told me.

(Nelson sits behind Maria straddling her. He rubs a half-bitten apricot on her ribs and arms.)

NELSON: Did you know that the raw pits of bitter apricots contain small amounts of cyanide and that excessive consumption can kill you?

MARIA: Which ones are these . . . bitter or sweet?

NELSON: I think bitter.

(Maria pushes his hand away. He takes another bite from the apricot. Beat.)

MARIA: Do you want to go? Time is up.

NELSON: I don't care.

MARIA: Me either.

NELSON: I think I was born . . . a hundred years too late.

MARIA: Nothing has really changed . . . I'm going to get dressed.

NELSON: No wait, once more. This time for sure, I can do it.

MARIA: Are you sure that you are ready, that you are up for it?

(Beat. Nelson removes his belt from his pants. He loops the belt around Maria's neck. He hangs on to the end of the belt and lies down. Maria straddles him. She grabs a small pistol that is hidden under one of the pillows and places it

on Nelson's stomach, along with the condom. She repositions the belt on her neck.)

MARIA: The end has come.

NELSON: It could be a beginning.

MARIA: Regardless.

NELSON: And when I'm done?

MARIA: You shoot yourself.

NELSON: In the face?

MARIA: Not the face.

NELSON: The temple?

MARIA: Better . . . But why?

NELSON: Our last good-bye—

MARIA: No, so we can say, I did it my way.

(Blackout.)

END OF PLAY

The A-Word

Linda Faigao-Hall

Developed at Find Your Voice (formerly Starfish
Theatreworks) under Gail Noppe-Brandon, AEA
Production, one of three plays called *Snapshots* by Diverse City
Theater Company, August 16–September 1, 2007, at Samuel
Beckett Theater, New York City. Directed by Gregory
Simmons. Cast: Beth—Melanie Nicholls-King;
Young Man—Antwan Ward.

CHARACTERS

> BETH, fifties, any ethnicity, introspective, strives for meaning in her life, open to possibilities, yet fearful, ambivalent.
>
> YOUNG MAN, early twenties, impulsive, spontaneous, lives only for the moment.

SETTING

> Beth's living room.

TIME

> The present.

•   •   •

At rise, there's Beth, pacing, an expectant hush hanging in the air, and an open picture album. A few beats. Young Man enters.

BETH: You're a day late.

YOUNG MAN: And whose fault is that.

BETH: *(An attempt at lightness.)* Well, come on. Don't be shy. Give me a kiss. *(Young Man does not.)*

BETH: Don't be that way. *(Showing him the album).* Look. Paul's birthday present. A picture album of my life . . . The best birthday present ever. It's so—

BETH/YOUNG MAN: *(Beth, gushing; Young Man, smirking)* Romantic! *(A beat.)*

BETH: He said he started it right after my surgery a year ago. *(Young Man grabs the album unceremoniously.)*

BETH: BE CAREFUL! *(A card falls from it. Young Man picks it up.)*

YOUNG MAN: *(Giving her the card.)* Read it to me.

BETH: "To my lovely Beth . . . the best is yet to be. Love, Paul."

YOUNG MAN: Wuss. So where is he?

BETH: He left this morning.

YOUNG MAN: Argument?

BETH: Just the opposite. We've never been closer.

YOUNG MAN: You're such a liar.

BETH: No, I'm not. *(Pause.)* I asked him to leave.

YOUNG MAN: You kicked him out, you mean.

BETH: No, I didn't kick him out. I merely said I needed some time to myself. *(Pause.)* We need to talk.

YOUNG MAN: So what else is new? *(Studying the pictures.)* Everyone's here . . .

BETH: He was so thorough. Even tracked down an old picture postcard of my high school . . . they tore it down to make way for a superhighway years ago . . . Grandma Rose . . . I don't even know how he got hold of that one . . . A whole year, he's been doing it . . . and not a word . . .

YOUNG MAN: *(Turning a page.)* Even Brian's rock band. You hated that band.

BETH: No, I didn't.

YOUNG MAN: He was a lawyer.

BETH: The world has enough unhappy lawyers.

YOUNG MAN: He was no happy rocker either. Miserable punk. All coked up screwing nymphets and slapping you around.

BETH: That doesn't hurt anymore. I'm over it. I'm entitled to one mistake.

YOUNG MAN: You mean two. Two mistakes.

BETH: One. *(Joining him.)* Oh. Look . . . I was so thin . . . such a lovely bride . . . even I would say so myself.

YOUNG MAN: You look OK. Married twice . . . practice makes perfect.

BETH: You always include Steve. I told you. He doesn't count! I mean I wasn't married to him. *(Pause.)* I'm sorry, but I wasn't.

YOUNG MAN: So why does Brian count?

BETH: Because we were married.

YOUNG MAN: But he was an asshole.

BETH: Hey—

YOUNG MAN: Your own words.

BETH: I've redeemed myself in Paul. He proposed. Last night.

YOUNG MAN: Sounds like good news.

BETH: Isn't it?

YOUNG MAN: So what's the problem?

BETH: Problem? What problem? Can't I simply share the good news?

YOUNG MAN: Will you give it up?

BETH: He's proposed; he asked me to marry him—last night. I told him I need some time to think it over. I wanted to talk to you first. Don't spoil this one. You always ruin everything. But this time it's different. I'm in love with him. I feel loved.

YOUNG MAN: How do you know what it means to be loved?

BETH: You've changed. Over the years. You've gotten so—malignant.

YOUNG MAN: I've always been honest.

BETH: But it's true. I've never been happier.

YOUNG MAN: LIAR! The truth is, you're going to mess it up somehow because you're scared shitless. You've always been scared and you always blame me.

BETH: I want peace. I want peace. I'm not the same person I was the last time you were here.

YOUNG MAN: Then prove it!

BETH: Once, a rabid agnostic. Now look at me. I've developed a spiritual life I didn't think I was capable of finding. A devout Catholic. There's something to be said for surviving cancer. Last year, I didn't know I'd be around to celebrate it. Now I live each day as if it were my last and mean it.

YOUNG MAN: Except when it comes to me.

(He sweeps the album aside. Beth leaps to her feet and retrieves it.)

YOUNG MAN: There are no pictures of me. You still haven't told Paul about me! So what's so different this time?

BETH: Be reasonable. How can I have pictures of you?

YOUNG MAN: He's got one of Steve. You said he didn't count.

BETH: It's a class picture, for God's sake. Of course Steve would be in it. I knew it. Why can't you leave me alone!

YOUNG MAN: *(Laughing.)* But it's you who call me. And always the same words! And I say, OK. Send me back. Go on. Do it!

BETH: You think I can't? *(Pause.)* Get out. GET OUT!

YOUNG MAN: All right.

(Young Man turns around to go, but there is no conviction in it. He's been here before. Beth stifles a cry. Young Man stops in his tracks.)

YOUNG MAN: Aren't you tired of it? I am. This Paul. I believe he's different. I know he's in love with you, and you're in love with him. He nursed you back to health. He's patient. He's fucking good in bed. In fact, I'm surprised.

BETH: Why? I don't deserve him, you mean? I don't believe my luck? I better not blow this one or I'll never meet another man like him? Is that what you mean?

YOUNG MAN: How about children. Does he want any?

BETH: No. He's got his own. All grown up.

YOUNG MAN: So he's perfect. *(Pause.)* You're still running out of time. Finish it.

BETH: That's what Paul said. He said exactly those words. Except it's he who's running out of time. It's now or never, he said.

YOUNG MAN: Maybe something different will happen this time around.

BETH: What are you going to do?

YOUNG MAN: I don't know yet. It will come to me.

BETH: The words. Not the same words. You always say the same things. *(Pause)* Perhaps after I've had my coffee. I'm not human before I have my coffee.

YOUNG MAN: NO! Absolutely not! That's how it starts. A drink. Coffee. There's always something! Next thing you know, I've got to get the hell out of here and nothing will have been accomplished.

BETH: You're right.

YOUNG MAN: Good. Why don't *you* start? For a change.

BETH: Are you sure?

YOUNG MAN: No. But do it anyway.

BETH: *(Haltingly.)* Mom and Dad were in the middle of the divorce and I was hanging out with Steve Michaels.

YOUNG MAN: *(As if chanting a nursery rhyme. Compulsive.)*
Stevie the Dickman.
Stevie the Prickman.

BETH: You said you'll try something different. You're always crude. I remember when you were younger. You were so sweet. Innocent. You were gentle.

YOUNG MAN: I was a baby. All babies are sweet and innocent. If they came out talking, no one would want them. *(As if chanting a nursery rhyme.)*
Stevie the Dickman.
Stevie the Prickman.

BETH: Stop it! He was your father!

YOUNG MAN: A no-good son of a bitch asshole father. You know what it's like. I have to be cruel in order to be kind.

BETH: But you're never kind.

YOUNG MAN: *(Daring her.)*
Stevie the Dickman
and Betsy the Slut.

BETH: *(Slapping him.)* Go to hell!
(Young Man grabs her arm and bites her hand. Beth screams in pain. Young Man steps back, and Beth grimaces, holding her hand.)

YOUNG MAN: Come on, you can do this one. You stood up to chemo.

BETH: I can't handle your rage.

YOUNG MAN: Frustration. That's what drives me. You weren't even in love with him. You didn't even enjoy it.

BETH: We were so young! I was nervous. A virgin. So was he.

YOUNG MAN: And stupid. You were both stupid.

BETH: What did we know?

YOUNG MAN: You should have known plenty. It was the eighties, for God's sake.

BETH: Please, why do you have to do it this way?

YOUNG MAN: It's called tough love. Happy birthday!

BETH: Stop. I can't go through with this. Please. Go. I'll leave it alone. I promise!

YOUNG MAN: But you can't leave it alone. I don't trust you anymore, don't you get it? Go on . . . you didn't know what to do . . . you were messed up—angry—confused.

BETH: I'll go back to therapy. I promise!

YOUNG MAN: You stopped that years ago. Don't you think I'd know that? *(Pause)* That small hick town—the only thing you were looking forward to in your life was getting away from there.

BETH: The only thing I lived for was to see the world. Leave everything behind. Mom and Dad. The yelling . . . the smell of drink . . . the filthy house . . .

YOUNG MAN: Stevie was the only thing that made it bearable. And then came summer of eighty-seven. What a bummer.

BETH: I had to go to New York. I couldn't take the risk of someone seeing me.

YOUNG MAN: But it took so long for you to make up your mind, by the time you went to New York—

(Beth covers her ears, starts making sounds to drown out Young Man's words.)

YOUNG MAN: We always stop here. I'm not going through this again. *(Beth turns to run, hands covering her ears. Young Man grabs her. They struggle. The fight is short but fierce. He pins her down, holds her face in a vice.)* YOU WERE PAST THE FIRST TRIMESTER! *(Silence.)* There. That's not so bad, is it? *(He lets her go. All the wind has gone out of her.)*

YOUNG MAN: What do you want?

BETH: I want you to stop haunting me.

YOUNG MAN: Don't you think that's up to you?

BETH: I want to be healed.

YOUNG MAN: Why? Were you wounded? It was your choice! You were free, weren't you? Don't you believe you were free?

BETH: Yes! But just because I was free it doesn't mean I didn't do anything wrong. Freedom and doing the right thing—sometimes they're not the same.

YOUNG MAN: What did you do that was so wrong? *(Silence.)* Beth? What did you do that was so wrong? *(Silence.)* You want me to say it? *(Silence.)* Say it. Say it!

BETH: *(For Beth, like pulling teeth.)* I killed you. I flushed you out of my body. You had a heart and lungs and eyes and ears—the guilt—no one ever talks about the guilt—the waste of it—what could have been . . . *(Weeping now.)* Since then, I think that everything in my life that didn't work came from that one single wrong. God was punishing me. That's why Brian abused me . . . I deserved it. That's why lovers came and went . . . I deserved it. . . . I had cancer . . . I deserved it. Even now I feel I'm not worthy of Paul.

YOUNG MAN: Give me a proper burial.

BETH: What?

YOUNG MAN: Give me a proper burial.

BETH: I don't know what you're saying.

YOUNG MAN: *(Pause.)* I don't either. Just popped out. This is scary . . .

BETH: You're scared. You?

YOUNG MAN: We've never gone this far before. Hold me.

(They hold each other.)

BETH: What do we do now?

YOUNG MAN: *(Softly.)* Boy or girl?

BETH: What?

YOUNG MAN: Boy or girl? *(Pause.)* Choose.

BETH: A boy. You were always a boy.

YOUNG MAN: What do I look like? *(Pause.)* Choose.

BETH: *(Pause.)* You've got big, brown eyes . . . Stevie's smile . . .

YOUNG MAN: What's my name?

BETH: I don't know . . . I never—

YOUNG MAN: Give me a name. Choose.

BETH: David.

DAVID: Cool. I like it. David . . .

BETH: I'm sorry I never got to love you. Forgive me.

DAVID: I forgive you.

(Beth gives him a kiss, cradling him as they both close their eyes, rocking each other. A few beats.)

BETH: I'm sorry I don't have a picture of you.

DAVID: But you're right. I was never there. So let it be.

BETH: What?

DAVID: *(Reaching for the book.)* Everything in this book has brought you here . . . to this very moment . . . change one thing . . . change one tiny thing and you wouldn't be right here now . . . you wouldn't have met Paul . . . this man who loves you—this loving patient man who promises you the best is yet to be.

(He turns to go.)

DAVID: Have a good life. Good-bye, Beth

BETH: Good-bye, David.

> (*David exits. There is absolute and total silence. Then the telephone rings. Beth picks it up.*)

BETH: Hello . . . hi, Paulie. Why didn't you wake me this morning? . . . It was a lovely dinner party . . . yes . . . it's the best gift ever . . . it's right here . . . In fact I've been going over it all morning . . . you do know me so well . . . hurry home, my sweet, hurry home . . . the best is yet to be . . . (*Fade out.*)

END OF PLAY

Bride on the Rocks

DAVID WIENER

Produced Lamplighters One-Act Play Festival,
La Mesa, California (previous version at the
Lyceum Theatre, San Diego, July 2006), October 2007.
Directed by Lia Metz. Cast: Lloyd—David Rethoret;
Andrea—Michelle De Francesco.

LLOYD, a five-star mixologist with a lifetime of experience behind the very best bars. Past retirement age but not inclined to hang up his martini shaker.

ANDREA, Thirty-ish, midthirties, thirty-something, well, let's not get too specific. All ready to march down the aisle.

SETTING

A bar at a luxury hotel. For economy's sake, this can be two stepladders and a board, covered by a black drape.

TIME

The present: Andrea's wedding day, late in the afternoon.

• • •

At rise: The opening music covers the dark time while the set is being changed. As the music ends, the lights come up on Andrea, resplendent in a flowing white wedding gown, seated on a bar stool in front of Lloyd. He mans the bar like he's on the bridge of a battleship. Andrea's little veil is perched crookedly on top of her head. She drains a shot glass of tequila and carefully sets it down next to several others on the bar. She squeezes her eyes shut— and then has the distinct and unpleasant sensation she's being stared at. She looks over her shoulder, out toward the audience (and the unseen bar patrons).

ANDREA: —What're you looking at? *(Louder.)* What are you looking at?
LLOYD: Miss, please don't shout—it upsets the drunks.
ANDREA: *(Menacing pause, her eyes narrowing.)* *What* did you call me?
LLOYD: Nothing, I didn't call you anything. Look, just relax, OK—
ANDREA: Oh, no, no, no, no—oh, yes you did. What'd you just call me?
LLOYD: I didn't call you anything; I always make it a rule to say nothing that could possibly be construed as offensive in any way—
ANDREA: *(Seething, leans forward.)* How—did you—*address* me?
LLOYD: Uhmn—*address* you?
ANDREA: Yeah.
LLOYD: Uh—
    (Thinks hard.)—"Miss"?
ANDREA: Yeah. "Miss." *That's* what you called me. *(Holds her arms out, displaying her wedding gown.)* Are you BLIND?! Twelve hundred dollars

worth of silk-faced satin crying out, "Call me Mrs.!" And you call me "*Miss*"?! *(Taps the bar.)* Set me up again, blind man . . .

LLOYD: *(Pouring another shot for her.)* I beg your pardon. Congratulations on your marriage.

ANDREA: I'm *not* married. *(Drinks half the shot.)* He never showed up.

LLOYD: Oh.

ANDREA: "Oh" is right. "Oh," indeed, indeedy-do. Eighty-three guests sitting up there in the Cabeza del Sol room, whispering and wondering what's going on, for crying out loud. Salmon-mousse roulettes and champagne my dad can't really afford even though it's from Australia and taupe-and-emerald centerpieces and people from out of state—and *no groom.* Something old, something new, something borrowed, something blue, and something really strange—there ain't no groom! You got it?

LLOYD: I got it, I got it.

ANDREA: Oh-h-h-h-h-h—*YEAH* . . .

(Andrea suddenly grabs at her crooked veil, struggles with it, snatches it off her head, and slams it down onto the bar. Pause, maybe two full beats, as she glares at it. Suddenly, she brings her fist down onto the veil, hitting it half a dozen times, hard and fast. Lloyd stands back, not sure what to do.)

ANDREA: *(She smoothes the veil pityingly, with both hands.)* Poor bridal veil. Poor li'l thing. It's not your fault . . . *(Pause. Andrea slams her fist down onto the veil another three or four times and throws back the rest of her shot.)*

LLOYD: *(Desperately trying to make conversation.)* I—uh, you know, I read somewhere that the veil, it started out as a disguise in pagan weddings, see, so evil spirits couldn't recognize the bride and hurt her.

ANDREA: *(Glances up at Lloyd for a moment, then holds the veil up and looks at him through the sheer material.)* Well, *that* explains it—I shoulda had this made out of canvas. *(Andrea sticks the little veil back on her head, all crooked.)* How do I look?

LLOYD: You are a very beautiful young lady.

ANDREA: Oh, yeah, I'm a regular vision of loveliness. *(Andrea suddenly thinks of something; she rummages in her purse and pulls out a cruise-ship travel packet. Accusingly, almost like it's Lloyd's fault.)* Boarding documents for an eight-day honeymoon cruise, leaving at five PM tomorrow. What am I supposed to do with this *now*? *(Andrea stuffs the packet back into her purse.)*

LLOYD: *(By God, he almost feels like it IS his fault.)* Well—you could still go.

ANDREA: Alone?! What are you, nuts?!

LLOYD: *(Pause.)* No, blind.

ANDREA: *(Deep sigh.)* Oh, boy, it'll be *great* Monday morning when I'm back at work. I know exactly what I'll hear. Carol will do forty-five minutes about how "Men are just pigs." And Maria will shake her head and tell me she'll light a candle for me.

(Pause.)

LLOYD: You know, I used to date a Maria, years ago. She was an exotic dancer. It didn't work out. Later, I heard she got a good job with the fire department. All that experience with poles, I guess.

ANDREA: *(Looks at him and grins.)*—You're kidding, right?

LLOYD: *(Grins back at her.)* Yeah, just trying to make you smile.

(Andrea's grin vanishes as an awful thought wells up and starts her crying.)

LLOYD: Easy, take it easy . . .

ANDREA: *(Trying to talk and cry at the same time.)* I—don't wanna—have to— DATE—again!!

(Lloyd sets a box of Kleenex down on the bar. Andrea nods "thank you," grabs a handful of tissues, and manages to hold her crying down to a wet snuffle.)

ANDREA: And, oh—and my mom—I just can't wait to hear what she'll have to say. *(Imitating her mother.)* "I don't understand what you possibly could have done to scare him off. You're every bit as pretty as a lot of other women your age. It's a mystery to me, I just wish somebody would please tell me what it is that's *wrong* with you . . ." *(Taps the bar.)* The same . . .

(Lloyd pours her another shot.)

ANDREA: I don't know, it's just—you reach a certain age and you look back— and you see all these forks in the road behind you. Hundreds of forks in the road. And there are no "do-overs." You look back at all the paths chosen and all those roads not taken, and you see all those forks stretching back to the day you decided what kind of popsicle you liked best, and you realize that your life is all—forked up.

(Silence; Andrea stares off into the middle distance.)

LLOYD: Let me tell you something. If you ever meet someone who says they have no regrets—*run.* Only a serial killer has no regrets. I've been married three times, I regret 'em all. And back when I was young, I wanted to play football, but I couldn't get into the pros no matter how hard I tried and, boy, did I ever try. I wasted a lot of time chasing a mirage. I regret that, too. But you live and you learn. Right?

ANDREA: *(Nodding.)* . . . right.

(Andrea throws back the tequila. Then she looks at the empty shot glass and brings it up to her eye.)

ANDREA: Ohhh, no. I didn't get the worm in that one, did I? Please tell me I didn't drink the worm?

LLOYD: No, no, no.

(Andrea heaves a great sigh of relief.)

LLOYD: You drank the worm five shots ago.

ANDREA: Gaaaa! Aaagh! Beer nuts, gimme beer nuts!!!

(Lloyd quickly puts a bowl of beer nuts in front of Andrea, and she wolfs down a handful.)

LLOYD: He won't hurt you, believe me. There's lots worse in your average chocolate bar.

ANDREA: (Returning to her previous "Tequila buzz.") I suppose so . . . (Pause.) Do you like what you're doing now? Or do you regret this, too?

LLOYD: This? For someone with my personality, it's a good line of work to be in. I got hurt playing sports, so I learned how to tend bar. (Holds up his wrist.) Compound fracture of the wrist.

ANDREA: From football?

LLOYD: No, when I finally gave up on football, a guy I knew got me some work in professional wrestling. I told myself, well, at least it's a pro sport. Sort of.

ANDREA: Were you on TV?

LLOYD: No, I helped train the TV wrestlers. The Freddie Blassie types, those guys. Like a fight arranger. Everybody thinks it's fake, which it is, but you can really get hurt doing that fake stuff. I was working with a wrestler called Paulie the Pinhead and I just wrecked my wrist.

ANDREA: What happened?

LLOYD: Well, Paulie the Pinhead was not a great one for preparation. He wanted to stumble into you and just wing it, you know, ad-lib. I tried to tell him, "Look, Paulie, this is not Friday night at the improv, OK? In pro wrestling, we have to choreograph things." But the guy really was pretty much a pinhead. He wouldn't listen. So he moved wrong, and I moved wrong, and I messed up my arm. I decided it was time to learn another trade, so here I am.

ANDREA: Did Paulie the Pinhead get hurt, too?

LLOYD: Him? Nah—he's like the drunk in a car wreck. Everybody else gets turned to hamburger, and he just walks away, whistling.

(Pause. Andrea starts to sway and looks very green.)

ANDREA: Oh. Oh-h-h-h-h . . .

LLOYD: Are you gonna throw up?

ANDREA: Oh-h-h-h-h-h . . .

LLOYD: Are you? Because if you are, I'll take you to the toilet. You don't want to upchuck all over your nice white dress.

ANDREA: *(Fighting for control.)* I am *not* going to heave . . .

LLOYD: Might do you some good, you know.

ANDREA: *No.* I am *not* going to ralph . . .

LLOYD: It'll be over real fast, I promise. I've done it plenty of times, I know. I'll even hold your head.

ANDREA: *(Digging in her heels like a little kid.)* No.

LLOYD: Why not?

ANDREA: Because if I puke, I'll start to sober up. And I'd rather *die* than sober up . . . *(The nausea passes. Pause.)* Are people still looking at me?

LLOYD: Well, kind of. You don't often see somebody in a wedding dress sitting at a bar, knocking back tequila shots.

ANDREA: Well, let 'em look. I'm not a dried-up old prune, yet. I'm still a plum. Right?

LLOYD: Right. And you look great in that dress.

ANDREA: Yeah, but I'm getting rid of it.

LLOYD: Really?

ANDREA: Yup. It's all stained.

LLOYD: *(Looks at the gown.)* Where?

ANDREA: *(Indicating different parts of the spotlessly clean dress.)* This one here— that's three weekends with my best friend and my mom going to all the bridal shops in town. And this over here—that's the Saturday we went out to a fancy lunch and looked at satin swatch books. And this is the Sunday we spent doing the fitting and alterations. The thing's a mess. Get it?

LLOYD: I got it, I got it.

ANDREA: So, hi-ho, hi-ho, it's off to eBay she goes. And may the next girl have better luck with her.

(Pause.)

LLOYD: You know, I really think you should go on your honeymoon.

ANDREA: By myself.

LLOYD: Sure, by yourself. Make it a vacation to get your head together.

ANDREA: Oh, what a great idea! I'll go on the Jilted Bride Tour.

LLOYD: Now, don't make it any worse than it is. You don't know that you were *jilted.* You were just stood up, that's all.

ANDREA: Thanks. I feel lots better now. *(Beat.)* . . . I know what's going to happen to me.

LLOYD: Look, you probably don't want to get started on that. I know things look grim right now but you have to remember that—

ANDREA: *(Like she doesn't even hear him.)*—I can see it all, plain as day . . .

(Lloyd slumps a little on the bar; this is not heading in a good direction.)

ANDREA: *(Trancelike.)* I'll get older and my hair will get bigger and higher and bluer. And I'll be a warning beacon to all the younger girls at the office. Like one of those World War II venereal disease posters: "*Don't* Let This Happen to *You!*"

LLOYD: *(He's trying to stop an express train.)* Look, there's no need to get all maudlin, you're still young and you've got all *kinds* of great things to look forward to—

ANDREA: *(Didn't hear a word.)* And I'll start to dress like an idiot. All kinda funny hats and weird shoes. And I'll be the one who gets stuck arranging the office birthday parties and the baby showers and the bridal showers because, well, it's nice to give her something special to do, you know, seeing how she's alone and all.

LLOYD: *(Knows it's hopeless but keeps on swinging.)* How about a fresh pot of coffee? I've got all different flavored coffee, ladies love that stuff. I got vanilla bean, mocha frappe. I got caramel nut, I got—

ANDREA: *(Deep sigh.)* And I'll see 'em come and I'll see 'em go. And I'll watch the single girls get married and they'll drag their kids in on Bring Your Brat to Work Day.

LLOYD: I think I have some nice hot chocolate here. Peppermint hot chocolate! Now how's that, something special for a special girl—

ANDREA: *(Like he's not even there.)* And one day, I'll just keel over. And they'll only find me because of the smell. Lying on my back. "Help I've fallen and I can't get up." On the cold, hard, filthy kitchen floor. Dead'rn hell. Surrounded by my Victorian tea-cup collection. And my Happy-Thought-for-the-Day pot-holder collection. And my Soap-Opera-Stars salt-and-pepper shaker collection.

(Poor Lloyd is really wilting, now. He pours another shot of tequila, apparently for Andrea.)

ANDREA: The paramedics will break down the door . . . and they'll put their hands over their noses and think, "My God, how long has this poor soul been rotting away all alone in this miserable apartment?" And they will walk into the kitchen—and see my grinning skull, gazing heavenward.

LLOYD: Your *skull?*

ANDREA: *(Nodding thoughtfully.)* My starving cats will have eaten off my face. And the county authorities will take me away. And dump my body into a mass grave. Yeah.

LLOYD: They don't *have* mass graves anymore.

ANDREA: *(Shrugs—it's a minor detail.)* OK. A pauper's grave. With a little granite marker that says: "Here lies a cat lady known only to God." The Tomb of the Unknown Cat Lady.

(Lloyd throws back the shot of tequila.)

LLOYD: *(Wiping his mouth with his hand.)* That one's on the house . . .

ANDREA: The weeds and brambles will slowly cover that unvisited, neglected plot of ground. And, eventually, even the darling little sparrows and the gentle woodland creatures will avoid it.

LLOYD: *(Can't take this another second.)* OK, OK, OK!

(Andrea rouses a little but she's still plenty fuzzy.)

LLOYD: Let's move onto something else, now. How about a good old-fashioned bar bet?

ANDREA: . . . A bar bet?

LLOYD: I'll bet you— *(Lloyd takes a quarter out of his pocket and slaps it down on the bar. Then he picks up a shot glass and steps around to the front of the bar.)*— I bet you I can get that quarter back into my pocket *without* touching the shot glass. *(He places the shot glass upside down over the quarter.)* If I win, you have to stay here and keep buying expensive drinks from me.

ANDREA: And what if I win?

LLOYD: You take a cab home, sober up, and go on your cruise tomorrow. Deal?

ANDREA: *(Shrugs.)* You're on.

LLOYD: OK. *(Lloyd makes some fancy moves like a magician. Andrea leans forward to keep a close eye on him. Lloyd waves his hands over the glass. He leans from side to side, then stops dead. He smiles and looks at Andrea.)* Darn. Can't do it. You win.

ANDREA: You *cheated.* You wanted to lose and you took advantage of my— *(Swallows a belch.)* —diminished capacity.

LLOYD: Doesn't matter. You took the bet and you—won! You can't welsh on *winning.* *(Half a beat.)* So? What are you going to do?

ANDREA: What am I gonna do. *(A pause as she comes to a decision.)* I'm gonna go home— *(Gathering up the folds of her voluminous wedding gown.)* — and I'm going to sleep it off, and tomorrow, I'm going to get onto that ship and I'm gonna go on my honeymoon— *(A thought occurs to her and she stops gathering up her dress for a moment.)* Who knows? *(A beat.)* Maybe I'll meet someone.

(She looks at Lloyd and shrugs. She starts to leave, stops, walks back, and gives Lloyd a kiss on the cheek. She quickly walks away, exiting the stage. The closing music comes up as Lloyd goes back around the bar and takes up his post once again. As he busies himself with glasses, the lights fade to black.)

END OF PLAY

Cell Mates

Molly Best Tinsley

Cell Mates was a Maxim Mazumdar New Play Competition
Finalist. It premiered at Alleyway Theatre, Buffalo,
New York, 204. Directed by Joyce Stilson. Cast: Cass—Kim
Piazza; Rob—Kevin Brach. Also part of 10 by 10 in the
Triangle, at the ArtsCenter, Carrboro, North Carolina,
July 12–22, 2007. Directed by Emily Ranii. Cast: Cass—
Danielle Cappel; Rob—Cory Kraftchick.

SYNOPSIS

Telemarketer Cass decides to reach out and touch someone after gulling her own grandma knocks her thinking outside the box.

CHARACTERS

ROB, late twenties, telemarketer.
CASS, late twenties, ATT Telephone Sales Associate of the Month.

SETTING

Adjoining office cubicles.

TIME

The present.

•   •   •

At rise: Two cubicles, open to the audience but separated by a six-foot partition. Rob and Cass sit in front of computer screens wearing headphones. They are both talking, but we only hear Cass, picking her up in midsentence as she reluctantly closes a sale.

CASS: Whenever you're ready . . . 5-0-8-6 . . . 6-0-0-1 . . . You know, Mrs. Jones, on second thought, suicide bombers are really pretty rare in Kansas, and why would they be interested in an old double-wide next door to a junkyard anyway? Sorry. I was just being hypothetical. Sometimes when I talk to people, I get these pictures. *(Beat.)* Really? Well, I certainly didn't mean to insult your place of residence. Actually, I see a very cheery interior—lots of embroidered pillows and silk flowers. *(Beat.)* I guess it's just this gift I have. But my point is, nothing's going to happen in an out-of-the-way place like Parsons. *(Beat.)* Yeah, well, that guy was probably just smoking in bed or something. *(Beat.)* I really don't think *you* have a thing to worry about. *(Beat.)* Hey, I am *still* deeply committed to protecting the innocent, I'm just trying to be honest *(Sotto voce.)* for a change. When you stop and think, the chances of that stuff happening are about the same as getting bit by a rattlesnake in Ray's Food Mart. *(Beat.)* Ray's? What can I say? The picture came to me. And now it's no trouble at all to just void this whole transaction, if you would please, stop, and *think*, Grandma, I mean, Mrs.—*(Beat.)* I meant it as a compliment, Mrs. Jones. A term of respect. *(Beat.)* Fine. What's your expiration date,

I don't care. I mean, I'm sorry, of course I *care.* *(Beat.)* I'm deeply committed. Of course. It's been such a long day. I want to thank you for choosing A T and T, a name you can trust. And remember what Homeland Security tells us: *You can be afraid, or you can be ready!* *(Cass takes off her headset, drops her head into her hands with a loud groan.)* Oh God. I don't believe it.

(Rob glances at the partition, removes his headset, and while Cass agonizes, he unfolds a cell phone, which rings now on Cass's side, an electronic version of the turgid finale to Finlandia. *Cass sits up, shakes her head. Finally she pulls out her cell, flips it open, but remains silent.)*

ROB: Hello? . . . Cass? Everything OK over there? . . . Honey?

CASS: Oh for godsake, hello.

ROB: Well, if you're not going to be civil, we don't have to bother.

CASS: *(Loud.)* I'm being civil. *(Softer.)* I'm just beat, that's all.

ROB: Busy day?

CASS: Nonstop.

ROB: That's my fast-talking girl. How much did you sell?

CASS: I don't know.

ROB: *(Affectionately.)* Don't give me that.

CASS: I lost track.

ROB: What do you mean? You never lose track.

CASS: I think I'm going to be sick.

ROB: Wait a minute. I must have the wrong number. Is this Kick-ass Cass, Telephone Sales Associate of the Month?

CASS: It isn't fun anymore.

ROB: Come on, you can't tell me it wasn't fun winning that portable, high-definition, slim-line, water- and fireproof mini-TV you can prop anywhere?

CASS: Oh, Rob. I want a job I can feel proud of.

ROB: Well, hey, you're helping people feel secure.

CASS: I'm scaring the shit out of them first, till they're begging to have their houses wired and their perimeters planted with electric eyes.

ROB: Sometimes I think I never will.

(Cass's eyes shift to the partition.)

CASS: You don't *have* a house. How could you afford a house—on what we make?

ROB: I meant, feel secure. I wish I could, but I just don't. *(Accusing.)* You're looking in my direction. I can tell.

CASS: *(Eyes front again.)* Jeez. Rob, what's wrong with that? I mean you were sharing something *personal* about yourself.

ROB: Exactly. So why do you have to push it?

CASS: I wasn't pushing anything. I thought we were starting to have a real conversation, for once.

ROB: You were not looking my way with unconditional acceptance, I could tell. You were looking snoopily.

CASS: Snoopily? Give me a break. I just spent ten hours hooked up to a phone.

ROB: Me too.

CASS: So, when the day's over, I want to do something different. Explore new territory.

ROB: I say stick with what's familiar. Like two old pairs of slippers. Now that Big Brother Freeny's gone home and the clock's not running, we can just lean back and relax . . .

CASS: *(Loud.)* God, this is so depressing.

ROB: Maybe it's time you asked your doctor about Paxil.

CASS: I don't need Paxil.

ROB: There's no stigma, you know.

CASS: Besides, who can afford a doctor?

ROB: They say it's safe for four-year-olds, Paxil is. For parents who want their kids to be fun and cute 24/7, not just when they're sleeping.

CASS: I need a job where I can express my sensitive side. Do you think I could get a venture capitalist to back a poetry business?

ROB: Hey, sure. There's a big market for catchy jingles.

CASS: I could hire myself out to recite at bar mitzvahs, bridal showers, funerals. Like a caterer, except my fancy food would be food for *thought*.

ROB: All you need is a business plan, figure your costs, profit margin, channels for distribution. Exit strategy. Just treat it like anything else.

CASS: I was afraid of that.

ROB: What's the problem?

CASS: I'd want it to be different. *(Beat.)* Couldn't we talk face to face?

ROB: Cass. I can't think straight face to face, you know that.

CASS: But I need something to be different.

ROB: You just want to see me all off balance and tongue-tied.

CASS: Maybe what I really need is a hug.

ROB: *(Cringing.)* I didn't hear that.

CASS: How about we trade back rubs? *(Beat.)* That isn't face to face. We could both close our eyes. Rob?

ROB: *(Eyes closed.)* Mmm. You've just stepped out of the shower, all warm and flushed, and now you're stretching out on your stomach on a white satin sheet . . . and I'm smoothing some scented . . .

CASS: Not a phone back rub, dummy. I meant the real thing.

ROB: *(Snapping his phone shut.)* I don't need this abuse.

CASS: What? Rob? Don't hang up on me.

(She hits the partition. Rob stares straight ahead. She claws the partition, butts it with her head, knocks on it.)

CASS: You know, we *could* talk *through* this thing. I mean, it's thin as cardboard. Save those precious minutes on our regional cell plans. *(Beat.)* Don't be that way. *(Beat.)* OK. Never mind. I give up.

(She punches Rob's number. His cell rings with an electronic polka, "Roll Out the Barrel." He answers.)

ROB: You called me a dummy.

CASS: It was just a manner of speaking.

ROB: You like to make me feel inadequate.

CASS: No, I don't. I really, I don't know, the thing is, I think, you should, why can't you realize, hey, I really care about you.

ROB: That's easy for you to say.

CASS: So I don't see why we can't go in together on a nice little house with a front porch and maybe one of those swings on it.

ROB: I don't believe you're pushing it again.

CASS: After work, we could sit there side by side, creaking back and forth, maybe bring out some chips, a little salsa. Instead of this shit.

ROB: Well, excuse me if I happen to like it here, with everyone gone. I mean you can take your shoes off and skate down the hall to the john in your socks.

CASS: Well, it creeps me out. I'm going to Taco Bell.

(She clicks her phone closed, pulls out her backpack, and begins loading it. Rob looks around desperately, sets down his phone. They begin to talk at each other, through the partition.)

ROB: Don't leave, Cass. *(Beat.)* I told you I'm not used to bonding with *people.* They're so spongy and nondurable and glum.

CASS: I am not glum, I am lonely. And you are too.

ROB: What do you mean? I really look forward to this little breather at the end of the day. Recharge the old batteries. Share a little harmless chitchat about current events—

CASS: While our little lives flow right down the little drain.

ROB: You tell me the latest about Gwyneth Paltrow, and I tell you my picks for the Superbowl.

CASS: That's not current events. That's marshmallow fluff on Wonder Bread. That's lint from Uncle Sam's navel. Amber waves of astroturf.

ROB: *(Interrupting.)* Since when are you so negative?

CASS: I don't think you'd know a current event if it jumped out and bit you.

ROB: You've got to lighten up. Really. It's the American way.

CASS: Oh, Rob. I just talked to my grandmother.

ROB: There you go! That's the right idea.

CASS: No it wasn't. The right idea, not at all. The program dialed her number in Kansas, and I didn't realize. I mean, I'm on automatic pilot, she's just another Mrs. Jones, typical polite, lonely old woman, the usual neuron loss upstairs—so I launch into my pitch about the hordes of have-nots creeping out of the cities to pillage suburbia, the sullen unemployed lurking in the shadows of the 7-Elevens, the half-crazed crack addicts in ski masks—prying open a basement window.

ROB: God, you've gotten good.

CASS: Anyway, I trot out the whole line-up, illegal aliens to terrorists, and it doesn't dawn on me it's her till I'm closing the sale and she's hitting her Visa with way more than she can afford. And it *never* dawned on her it was me—I mean, she was the one who used to tell me, the sky's the limit for you, Cassie. You're going to zoom right up there and hang by your knees from the moon. How could I tell her where I am now and what I'm doing? God, I am so ashamed. How can I ever face her again?

ROB: *(Tentatively.)* Maybe it's time you asked your doctor about Xanax.

CASS: *(Pounding on the partition.)* I want a real life. It's like we've let ourselves be blinded by shiny trinkets while they've stolen all our land.

ROB: It's done wonders for me. Sure, it makes my mouth a little dry and it does take a major edge off the old sex drive, but then I can really focus on my work.

CASS: I guess the stupid part is I keep thinking I'd have the guts to grab some of it back, if you and I could just, I don't know, get it together . . . side by side, face to face.

ROB: *(Interrupting.)* That is definitely the stupid part.

CASS: *(Taking a deep breath.)* I have had it. *(She climbs up on her desk.)*

ROB: Had what?

CASS: It's now or never.

ROB: What? What is?

(She rises above the partition.)

CASS: Surprise, Rob. Look up here?

ROB: *(Snatching up his phone.)* I think you're breaking up.

CASS: We're the ones who'll be breaking up, Rob, if you don't look at me.
  (Rob does and drops his phone.)
ROB: Oh no. I don't . . . I tell you . . . I can feel . . . it's all, I mean, can't breathe. Allergic reaction. *(He grabs his headset and jams it on, then starts typing on his keyboard and clicking his mouse.)* I think I'm having chest pains. Uh oh. I'm going to crash.
CASS: *(One leg clearing the panel.)* Go ahead. We'll boot you up again.
ROB: You don't understand, I've still got numbers to call, deals to close, you can't push yourself in my space, I won't be me anymore.
CASS: *(Standing on his desk.)* All the better.
ROB: This is no time to make fun.
CASS: Finally, we agree. *(Beat.)* Look, I'll sit way over here on this end. *(Beat.)* I won't even look at you if you will just admit it. You're lonely too.
ROB: I can't handle this.
CASS: You don't know that.
ROB: You don't know me. I don't know you.
CASS: That's the good news.
  (Rob takes off his headset, picks up the cell phone, stares at it, then throws it down and regards Cass. She sneaks a peek.)
CASS: You look pretty good from the front. *(Beat.)* Then you say, *So do you.*
  (Rob nods. Cass has shifted to a seated position, legs hanging over the edge of the desk. Rob flinches away. She inches closer.)
ROB: You're on my side.
CASS: I'd like to be. Why don't you just pretend my eyes are two very small screens. And this hand's a mouse?
  (She touches his hand; he jumps.)
CASS: Easy does it. You want to scan for viruses, go ahead.
  (Holding his gaze, she inches closer.)
ROB: What's that smell?
CASS: *(Stretching her arm under his nose.)* What smell?
ROB: Sort of sweet?
CASS: Something spongy, nondurable, but very nice. Something you can definitely handle. All you want.

END OF PLAY

The Charm of the British

LAURA COTTON

First performed at Florida State University,
June 2007. Directed by Laura Cotton.
Cast: Kate Snefferfield—Robin Beale;
Rob Snefferfield—David Jacobson.

CHARACTERS

KATE SNEFFERFIELD, mid- to late twenties. A cheerful, imaginative person who isn't quite in touch with reality.

ROB SNEFFERFIELD, mid- to late twenties. Kate's husband. A seemingly gruff guy who has a sensitive side. He speaks in an English accent in the beginning of the play, an American accent in the middle, and a French accent in the end.

SETTING

The living room of the Snefferfield's home.

TIME

The present: around noon.

•   •   •

At rise: Rob sits in a chair, reading a magazine. Kate enters. She walks over to the chair next to Rob, picks it up, and moves it a few feet. Then she picks up a plant on the coffee table and moves it on the floor. Then she picks up a book, opens it, and replaces it exactly where it was. Rob watches all this.

ROB: *(With English accent.)* What in bloody day are you doing?

KATE: *(Jumps in surprise.)* Huh?

ROB: Why do you keep moving everything? Did the jitterbug bite your bottom?

KATE: Ha, ha. Very funny, Rob. Actually, I'm centering our room. I've been reading a book on feng shui, and this room is completely off balance.

ROB: *(Incredulous.)* The room is off balance?

KATE: Yes. Would you mind sitting over there? I think that would help.
(Rob shakes his head, moves over to where Kate pointed. Kate walks around the room, straightening pillows, moving magazines, repositioning books. Then she looks at Rob again, shakes her head.)

KATE: Sorry. I was wrong. It's worse with you over there. Can you go back to where you were?

ROB: *(Rob sighs, stands up, and goes back to sit in his original chair.)* Why do you always have to do this?

KATE: Do what?

ROB: Make us do completely asinine things. You get some loony idea in your head and then you get upset if we don't do it.

KATE: Like what? What are you talking about?

ROB: I can't believe you would even ask me that. Just yesterday you told me that we should become vegans. Vegans, Kate. Not even vegetarians. And all because you watched some blarmy special on PBS.

KATE: And I *still* think we should be vegans. All that milk and cheese can't be good for us.

ROB: And then, last week you wanted us to move to LA and become extras. Just out of the blue, because you suddenly had an urge to try your hand at acting.

KATE: *(Shrugging.)* It seemed like a good idea at the time.

ROB: And the week before that, you wanted to—what was it?—create your own workout video?

KATE: Now, that really *was* a good idea. I still might do that.

ROB: Every day, it's something different. It's like you're on some kind of road trip and you want to see all the sights before you die. Except *we* are the sights and no one's dying.

KATE: Everyone's dying, Rob. Little by little, each day, we're all dying.

ROB: Don't give me that crap, Kate. If you want to live in an eternal state of "I don't know who I am or what I want," that's fine. But leave me out of it. *(Beat.)*

KATE: This is horrible. We fight all the time now. We hate each other. And we can't agree on anything! And this room is still really off balance! *(Bursts into tears.)*

ROB: Nobody hates anyone. And the room is fine.

KATE: You see? We can't even agree on that! I knew this would happen. I knew our marriage would be one endless fight that would last for all eternity.

ROB: Come off it, Kate. You didn't know anything. If you did, you wouldn't have married me.

KATE: *(Bursting out.)* I didn't marry you! *(Beat.)*

ROB: *(Stunned.)* How'd you find out?

KATE: How'd I find out what?

ROB: Forget it. What were you going to say?

KATE: Our marriage isn't . . . It isn't valid. The pastor was . . . He was . . .

ROB: What?

KATE: He was a clown.

ROB: I don't remember him being all that funny.

KATE: No, no, you don't get it.

ROB: OK, actually I do remember him telling a joke or two. But it was hardly *Saturday Night Live.*

KATE: I mean, he was a real clown, Rob. *(Taking a deep breath.)* I called the real pastor a few days before the wedding and I canceled him. Then I looked in the yellow pages for an actor. Someone who could play the pastor at our wedding. But none of the actors in our area were available. They were all in the Renaissance Festival downtown. So I hired a clown instead. I had to pay him double his usual fee because he didn't have a costume.

ROB: Damn it, Kate. You've jumped the crazy train and you're steering at full speed.

KATE: It's true. It really is. You see, about two months before the wedding, I realized I wasn't ready. I felt like I didn't know you well enough. I felt like . . . like you were hiding something from me.

ROB: And you never thought to mention that to me?

KATE: I thought you'd get upset.

ROB: I am upset!

KATE: So you see, I was right. *(A beat.)* I'm so sorry, Rob. Can you ever forgive me?
(Silence.)

ROB: I'm not sure you should be apologizing . . . You see, the truth is, I *have* been hiding something. *(Takes a deep breath.)* My name really isn't Rob Snefferfield.

KATE: It's not?

ROB: *(Without English accent.)* No. My real name is Luke Laroche. And I moved here from Wisconsin.

KATE: But you have an English accent. Or had one anyway.

ROB: I made up the accent to meet women. American women are very attracted to British men.

KATE: You're kidding.

ROB: No, they really are. American women love British guys. Especially angry British guys. I read a study about it in a magazine. And I always wanted to be called Rob. So I decided to give it a go. I moved here and started introducing myself as Rob. People liked Rob. I liked Rob. And I had a great time pretending to be upset about everything.

KATE: You've been lying to me? All this time?

ROB: I never meant for it to last this long. I wanted to tell you before our wedding, but I just couldn't do it. I was afraid—I was afraid I'd lose you forever.
(A beat.)

KATE: *(Devastated.)* So that's why your family wasn't at our wedding. It wasn't because they couldn't afford the plane ticket. It was because they never knew about it.

ROB: Yes.

KATE: How could you? How could you deceive me for all this time?

ROB: I didn't know what else to do. And honestly, I never thought it would hurt you. I thought you liked me the way that I was.

KATE: I *loved* you the way that you were. Because I love the British. They're just so . . . So charming. Yes. That's the word, "charming." Everything about them is charming—their accents, their tea times, their strange little jokes that no one understands. My favorite group is and always will be the Beatles, and I've read eight and a half biographies on the royal family. *(Beat.)* I can't believe this. This is horrible.

ROB: We'll get through it, Kate.

KATE: No, no, you don't understand. I don't want to get through it. The only reason I married you is because I thought you were British.

ROB: You didn't marry me.

KATE: But I pretended to! If you're not British, I don't see how this is going to work. The only thing that kept me going was the idea that you were British. *(In a dreamy, dramatic voice.)* And that someday we would travel to England and I would meet the Queen—

ROB: I never said I knew the Queen.

KATE: It's a fantasy. Let me finish. *(Dreamy, dramatic voice.)* That someday we would travel to England and see the Queen and the Eiffel Tower—

ROB: The Eiffel Tower's in France.

KATE: I know that, Rob, of course I know that. I just thought that because England is so close to France that we would stop in. Anyway, *(Dreamy, dramatic voice.)* We would see the Eiffel Tower and walk along the Riviera—

ROB: The Riviera is also in France.

KATE: We're still in France in my fantasy, Rob. Try to keep up. *(Dreamy, dramatic voice.)* And we would end our trip with a personal tour of the Louvre.

ROB: That's in France too.

KATE: OK, so in addition to England, I like France. So what? Either one is much more interesting than America.

(Beat.)

ROB: Well, it's funny you say that, because *(With French accent.)* Je suis français.

KATE: Huh?

ROB: I'm French.

KATE: Yeah, right. You said you were from Wisconsin.

ROB: *(With French accent.)* No. I said I moved here from Wisconsin. I'm from France. And that's where my family still lives.

KATE: Really?

ROB: Really. How do you think I knew that all those places you named were in France?

KATE: That's a good point.

ROB: It's because I'm French. Like I said, my real last name is French. Laroche. Very French. And that's why I can speak French.

KATE: Really?

ROB: *Oui, mademoiselle.*

KATE: Wow! That's fantastic news. That's even better than you being English.

ROB: It is?

KATE: Of course. France is far, far more exciting than England.

ROB: I always thought French men were smelly and fat. At least that's the way all the guys in my family are.

KATE: No, no. French men are seductive and sophisticated. I can't believe you're French! This is so great. We have to go, we have to go to France immediately. Oh, and while we're there, we really should get married again! I'd love to be Mrs. . . . Mrs. . . . What did you say your last name was again?

ROB: Laroche.

KATE: Oh. Well, it's not exactly beautiful. But it's better than Snefferfield.

ROB: It sounds like a great plan, Kate. There's only one problem . . .

KATE: Oh no. What?

ROB: My family kinda . . . Well . . . This is hard for me to say, Kate.

KATE: Take your time.

ROB: *(Nods, takes a deep breath.)* They always wanted me to marry a French girl.

KATE: Oh.

ROB: But maybe you could pretend to be French.

KATE: Yes! I would love that. I've always wanted to be French. French women don't get fat, you know. Or is it thin? French women don't get thin? That sounds strange. But anyway, I'd love that.

ROB: You'd probably have to take a few language classes, you know, study the culture and all.

KATE: I could do that. I'm a wiz at taking classes.

ROB: It could take a while. Maybe a year or more.

KATE: Oh, that's fine. We have plenty of time. This is so exciting, Rob. This is way better than any other idea I've ever had.

ROB: I had the idea.

KATE: That's right. It was my idea and you had it for me. *(Looking at the audience and talking.)* Can you believe it? I've gone from pretending to be married to a British guy to becoming a French woman engaged to a French guy. *(Beat.)* Life just doesn't get any better than this!
(Lights fade.)

END OF PLAY

Drury Lane

DON NIGRO

CHARACTERS
JAMES RUMPLEY, perhaps forty.
JANE ARMITAGE, early twenties.

SETTING
The stage of David Garrick's Drury Lane Theatre in London. A piece or two of drab and worn dark furniture, perhaps, but nothing fancy. The stage is mostly bare, and the players are surrounded by darkness.

TIME
Some point in the mid-eighteenth century.

• • •

Lights up on the stage of Drury Lane Theatre. James Rumpley looks to be about forty, tall, powerfully built, once good-looking, now a bit gone to seed, and Jane Armitage, early twenties, still lovely but with some hard times visible on her face. Empty theater, late at night.

JAMES: So. Shall we rehearse?
JANE: We're always rehearsing. We never cease to rehearse.
JAMES: Except when we're performing.
JANE: There's very little difference, really.
JAMES: Nevertheless.
JANE: I've grown weary of rehearsal.
JAMES: We must rehearse or we'll never get it right.
JANE: It will never be right.
JAMES: We must get it right, or Garrick will dismiss us.
JANE: He won't dismiss us. He likes us.
JAMES: He likes you.
JANE: He likes you, too.
JAMES: He likes me, but he doesn't trust me. He finds me unreliable. Unpredictable. And nearly undirectable.
JANE: So do I.
JAMES: You don't trust me?
JANE: I have trusted you far too much in my life, and look where it's brought us.
JAMES: It's brought us to Drury Lane.

JANE: Everything brings us here. Everything ends up here. All things come to Drury Lane.

JAMES: Do you think I trust you?

JANE: I don't care.

JAMES: You do care.

JANE: I just want to rest.

JAMES: We can't rest. We must rehearse.

JANE: I've forgotten my lines.

JAMES: You haven't forgotten anything. You never forget anything.

JANE: It's you who never forget. You're a monster of remembrance. And you torment me.

JAMES: I torment you?

JANE: You know you do.

JAMES: And why do you think I torment you?

JANE: Because you're a fool.

JAMES: You're the one who went to Garrick.

JANE: He was our friend.

JAMES: You went to him behind my back.

JANE: I had no choice. You were too proud to go yourself. We needed his help.

JAMES: And he was kind enough to offer it.

JANE: He was very generous.

JAMES: And what did you give him in return?

JANE: Nothing.

JAMES: *(His fury bursting out suddenly, an accusation, grabbing her arms.)* WHAT DID YOU GIVE HIM IN RETURN?

(They look at each other for a moment. Then he lets her go.)

JAMES: Was that too much, do you think?

JANE: It's always been too much.

JAMES: I think so, too. I can feel that it's too much. So why can't I seem to stop myself from doing it that way?

JANE: You've always been the victim of passions beyond your control.

JAMES: And you're one of them.

JANE: One among many.

JAMES: The only one that ever mattered.

JANE: If it pleases you to tell yourself that.

JAMES: You know it's true.

JANE: Then why do you torment me?

JAMES: Because you went to Garrick.

JANE: Garrick might have saved you.

JAMES: Nobody is saved. We're all damned here.

JANE: You might have been saved. You were too proud to accept his help.

JAMES: I didn't need his help.

JANE: We needed his help. Your child needed his help. But you preferred to turn thief.

JAMES: Preferred? I preferred? Do you imagine I had a choice?

JANE: You had a choice, but your pride prevented you. Pride, and drink, and falling into low company.

JAMES: Low company? Falling into low company? I'm an actor. I AM low company.

JANE: You know the company I'm referring to.

JAMES: I was raised by carny people, for God's sake. I travelled in gypsy wagons with a freak show. And yet you professed to love me. An undirectable man. An actor twice your age. Why, with this multitude of faults which you never tire of enumerating, why in the name of God did you ever want me in the first place?

JANE: I don't know.

JAMES: Well, make something up.

JANE: Mr. Garrick frowns upon improvisation.

JAMES: Another reason he can't stand me. I've been making it up as I go along all my life. I am a hopelessly improvisational individual.

JANE: You're a fine actor when you put your mind to it. But some spirit of perversity gets into you and—

JAMES: I'm not the one who sold her soul for a few pieces of silver.

JANE: YOU'D RATHER BE A THIEF THAN ASK A FRIEND FOR HELP. YOU'D RATHER HANG FROM A GALLOWS. AND LOOK AT THE CONSEQUENCES: YOU'VE SACRIFICED YOUR WIFE AND CHILD TO YOUR STUPID, SELF-DESTRUCTIVE PRIDE.

JAMES: Now, that's too much.

JANE: It's the truth.

JAMES: It might be the truth, but it's too much. It sounds like a play.

JANE: To you, everything is a play. You've made yourself the tragic hero of your life, and your child suffers for it.

JAMES: I don't want to hear you preaching to me about my child.

JANE: I don't care what you want to hear.

JAMES: No, I expect you don't. (Pause.) Where is he now, I wonder?

JANE: He's gone across the ocean, to America.

JAMES: Gone to live amongst the savages, has he?

JANE: He's your son. What would you expect?

JAMES: What's he doing there?

JANE: Probably drinking and whoring, like his father.

JAMES: One can only hope. *(Pause.)* I don't like this scene. Can't we do something else?

JANE: We can't change it now.

JAMES: Why can't we? Who's to stop us? Garrick? Do you think old Garrick would try to stop us from rewriting this scene a bit?

JANE: We can't rewrite the scene. We can only play it.

JAMES: So you're enjoying it, are you?

JANE: I hate it. I just want to rest. But there is no rest for us.

JAMES: What about the seduction scene?

JANE: Oh, God, no.

JAMES: Why not? It's the best scene in the play.

JANE: It's too painful.

JAMES: You seemed to be enjoying it while it was going on.

JANE: I was a fool.

JAMES: Yes. You were a fool. An innocent girl from the country, come to London to be on the stage.

JANE: Stop it.

JAMES: The theater, you know, child, does not have the greatest reputation as a place of high moral character.

JANE: I don't want to do this.

JAMES: You're improvising, Jane. Garrick wouldn't like that.

JANE: Do you slander your own profession? Then you slander yourself.

JAMES: I'll be buried in unconsecrated ground, and so will you, if you choose this for a life. You're better off to leave now while you still can.

JANE: I can't. My family will disown me. I've nowhere else to go.

JAMES: Yes. We are all drawn here by our desperation. I have loved and hated much in this place. All innocence is deflowered here.

JANE: It seems to me a very innocent place, in fact. A kind of holy place. Can you work here and not feel that?

JAMES: What do you want from this, girl? Do you want an easy life? Because you'll work like a dog. Do you want to be loved? Because one night they may seem to love you, but you can't take that love home with you, and the next night they'll be calling for your head on a platter. Do you want respect? Because you'll be viewed as a whore by respectable people everywhere.

JANE: Is that how they view you?

JAMES: Of course it is. A whore is paid to counterfeit an act of love. That's exactly what we do.

JANE: Do you enjoy destroying all my hopes? Hurling mud upon my dreams?

JAMES: Your hopes are unreasonable. Your dreams are not real. This sordid profession will use you up and kill you.

JANE: Then what are you doing in it?

JAMES: For me, the theater is an exquisite form of suicide.

JANE: Then I've come here to die with you.

(They look at each other. He kisses her, very tenderly. Pause.)

JAMES: You're right. We must not do the seduction scene.

JANE: Why not?

JAMES: It was the scene of your deflowering.

JANE: By you.

JAMES: Yes, God help me.

JANE: We've begun the scene. We might as well finish it.

JAMES: No. I've changed my mind.

JANE: You can undress me, and bed me on a pile of costumes.

JAMES: No. I don't want to.

JANE: Come on. We must rehearse. You said we must rehearse.

JAMES: I was weak. I should have driven you away.

JANE: You tried. I wouldn't listen. I wanted you. I wanted this. I still want it now. Do it again now. Do it again. Deflower me.

JAMES: It's a thing that only happens once.

JANE: Not in the theater.

JAMES: Get away from me. Have you no shame?

JANE: I married you. There's your answer.

JAMES: I remember you said to me after, lying together naked, you said, When I die, I want to haunt this place.

JANE: Did I say that?

JAMES: A theater is a very dangerous location. A person must be careful what they say there. You say it, and then it happens to you.

(Pause.)

JANE: Do you think this is Hell, then?

JAMES: No. Too drafty. Purgatory perhaps. And yet you know, there could be worse things. Worse punishment, if this is that.

JANE: What we've done is our punishment.

JAMES: I think what it is. I think at the moment of death, love sets going these strange loops in the brain. And they play over and over. Because all love leads to suffering, and suffering feeds off itself, it makes strange loops, and one gets trapped in them. There's no help for it. It's the play one is cast in. The dead haunt, and in turn are haunted. All places are haunted. But theaters are the most haunted places of all. That's why we come. *(Pause.)* This is the play. I was a carnival boy who became an actor. You were an innocent girl from the country, come to the theater. We made love on this stage one night. You were with child. I drank away what little we had. I was too proud to ask Garrick for help. You went and I hated you for it. I became a thief. I was caught and hung. You watched my public hanging with our son. And then you died.

JANE: And then I died.

JAMES: And the boy stowed away on a boat and went across the ocean. And here we are. Rehearsing the play. Again and again. Forever, in this place.

JANE: When I die, I said, I want to haunt this place.

JAMES: And so you have. And so you do.

JANE: It's a rather beautiful story, actually.

JAMES: Do you think?

JANE: We might make a play of it, you and I.

JAMES: We might. We have. We will.

JANE: There are worse fates than this.

JAMES: I expect. *(Pause.)* Do you think our son will be an actor?

JANE: Of course he will. Everybody is.

JAMES: Then God forgive him. And God forgive me. Or, the hell with God. Will you forgive me?

JANE: At the end of the play, perhaps.

JAMES: So. Shall we rehearse?

JANE: We're always rehearsing. We never cease to rehearse.

> *(They look at each other. The light fades on them and goes out.)*

END OF PLAY

Einstein + the Angels

Laura Harrington

Originally performed in the Boston Theater
Marathon, May 20, 2007. Produced by Publick
Theatre, Boston. Directed by Jason Slavick.
Cast: Jack—Rob Najarian; Abby—Lordan Napoli.

CHARACTERS
    JACK, fifteen.
    ABBY, fifteen.

SETTING
    The outskirts of a ruined city.

TIME
    The future.

NOTE: Jack and Abby should be played by adult actors.

•   •   •

At rise: Jack, dressed in ragged clothes, digs through a large pile of trash. The light is angled, gray, strangely opaque.

JACK: *(Impatiently tossing things over his shoulder.)* Cell phone—Blackberry—Beanie Baby—Pager—Hand grenade— *(We hear an explosion offstage.)* Whoops. *(Continuing.)* Girl Scout cookies— *(Shakes box, it's empty, tosses it.)* Doorbell— What day is it? Damnit! Is that so much to ask? Monday? Tuesday?
    (Abby, also ragged, glides in on a beat-up Razor scooter or a single skate and zips around the pile of trash.)
ABBY: Hey, Jack! Whatcha doin'?
JACK: Looking for stuff.
ABBY: Like what?
JACK: A calendar. A watch that still works. *Paper!*
ABBY: Havin' any luck?
JACK: Not yet.
ABBY: Hey! Let's do that electric thing.
JACK: *(Still searching.)* We did that yesterday.
ABBY: Last week.
JACK: Really?
ABBY: Yeah.
JACK: What day was *that?*
ABBY: I dunno.
JACK: Was it a good day or a bad day?

ABBY: *(Starts zipping back and forth on her razor.)* Hey! You want to get pregnant?

JACK: Do *I* want to get pregnant?

ABBY: Nooo . . . Me, silly. Us.

JACK: Are you kidding?

ABBY: Nooooo . . .

JACK: We're carcinogenic—

ABBY: We are *not!*

JACK: Or radioactive—

ABBY: —You're just sayin' that—

JACK: We're lucky we're not jelly. Or dust. Or—

ABBY: —You are *such* a downer.

JACK: I just want to know what day it is.

ABBY: *C'mon*—Let's do that thing—

JACK: I'm depressed.

ABBY: It'll make you feel better—

JACK: No, it won't—

ABBY: Yes, it will!

JACK: *(Turns back to rummaging through the trash.)* Does *anybody* know what day it is? *(Flinging stuff with fury.)* Flashlight—Fishing rod—Barbie doll—Passport—Checkbook—

ABBY: *(Rides over to Jack and flings herself on the pile of trash.)* Find me! Me! Me! ME!

JACK: Abby—

ABBY: C'mon. I need a little cuddle. *(A beat.)* Just a little cuddle? . . . A little one? A little . . . little one . . . ? Come on . . . Jack . . .

JACK: *(He lies down beside her; she immediately begins to climb on top of him.)* Hold on! Slow down!

(She freezes.)

JACK: Jesus! Not so fast. You gotta start slow. You got that?

ABBY: Slow is not my style.

JACK: Slow. Real. Real. Slow.

(She lies next to him, without touching him. He raises one finger—she grabs his whole hand. They both pull back quickly, as though they've been burned.)

JACK: Shit! Would you take it easy? *One* finger. *One.* At a time.

(They each raise one finger and touch again. We hear "bzzzzzzt" and see a strong current pass down each of their arms. They pull apart.)

ABBY: Wow.

JACK: OK. You OK?

ABBY: *(Delighted.)* Uh-huh.

JACK: That's not so bad.

ABBY: I like it, Jack.

(*They touch two fingers again: bzzzzzt.*)

ABBY: I like it a lot.

(*They pull apart.*)

JACK: Well, you're nuts.

ABBY: It doesn't happen with just anybody, you know. And other people? They can go to sleep at night, too. I've seen them—

JACK: You have not—

ABBY: They close their eyes. They sleep. They snore. They *fart.* They dream. And everybody's having sex left and right and they don't have to be careful, or slow . . . And there's no sparks—no "bzzzzt!"—all the time. And the whole room does not smell like a *fireplace* afterwards!

JACK: How do you know all this?

ABBY: And the angels? The angels are watching us. Hovering. And watching. In their tattered clothes. Covered with soot. They look like shadows.

JACK: Abby. You're dreaming—

(*He touches one finger—bzzzzzt—then takes her hand. We hear a crackle and see a puff of smoke.*)

ABBY: I'm very awake in my mind, Jack. Very, very awake. I think that's why I like touching you so much. And the current—or the music—or whatever it is—running from me to you—It's like the coolest thing I've ever heard of. How did we find each other? You think it's like fate? Or magnets? Or—Or—

JACK: —You are a very strange girl.

(*He pulls her close. Lightning flashes across the sky.*)

ABBY: These are very strange times.

(*She snuggles into him—more lightning.*)

JACK: Do you think there are the same number of hours in the day? Do you think we'll ever see the sun again? Or the moon? Do you think anything can grow without sunlight? Could we make a clock? Could we reinvent time?

ABBY: The angels say—

JACK: Oh, c'mon, Abby—there are no *angels*—

ABBY: Just because *you* can't see them—

JACK: Nobody can see them!

ABBY: You don't know that!

JACK: What you're seeing—or think you're seeing—Could be a vibration in

the air—Or a last vestige of someone who—someone who . . . (died).
Or—or—

ABBY: —angels.

JACK: Listen to me! We don't need fantasy. We need facts. And I'd like a clock
and a calendar and a power source. And some food.

ABBY: The angels say we don't need any of that stuff.

JACK: Right. Live on air.

ABBY: It's the last day, Jack.

JACK: It is not.

ABBY: The aftershock—

JACK: What aftershock?

ABBY: —Has not hit yet.

JACK: What are you talking about?

ABBY: Every action has an equally powerful reaction. Or something like that.
The aftershock. The reaction.

JACK: You're making this up.

ABBY: So I thought we could do that electric thing. Skateboard a little. Have
some more . . . y'know—before we . . . And then we could talk about
stuff we like, like blue skies and green grass and surfboards and rock and
roll and Mozart, even. I thought you could sing me a little something.
In your scratchy voice. And maybe tell some jokes. Some dumb chicken
jokes. And we can make up the perfect meal. Corn on the cob and devil
dogs and birthday cake with candles and a cold glass of milk. And then
you can hold me. And we can make sparks for a little while. To light up
the darkness. Whaddya say? Could we maybe do that?

(Ash begins to sift down from the sky like snow.)

ABBY: Oh! Look! Snow! *(She gets up, begins to twirl around in the "snow.")* And
it's not even cold— *(Sticks her tongue out, trying to catch flakes of "snow."*
She stops, spits, disgusted.) Agh! . . . Yecchhh! It's ash—

(Realizing what this means, she turns to Jack. We hear a dull rumble, like
thunder in the distance. They reach out to hold hands—bzzzzzt, crackle,
bzzzzzt—and, holding hands, watch the sky for a moment. Pause.)

JACK: I found a pen yesterday.

ABBY: Nice.

JACK: A Sharpie.

ABBY: Cool. I loved Sharpies. I had a whole collection.

JACK: So, Abby? Right here on your shoulder—I'm gonna write your name
and your date of birth. OK?

ABBY: OK.

JACK: In case anybody ever—y'know—

ABBY: Finds us—

JACK: Yeah.

(He kneels next to her and writes on her shoulder. We hear low-level crackly static as he writes.)

ABBY: Make it nice.

JACK: Quit wiggling!

ABBY: Now let me do you— (She writes his name: more static.) What's your birthday?

JACK: June sixteenth, 1995—

ABBY: Hey! It could be your birthday right now!

(She finishes writing, then leans in and kisses him: We hear sudden, rushing wind.)

ABBY: Wow! (She kisses him again: more wind.) Let's take our clothes off—

JACK: Abby—

ABBY: Don't be scared—They could be wrong, y'know—

JACK: Who?

ABBY: Einstein. And the angels.

JACK: The spectral bodies.

ABBY: Maybe I'm a spectral body. (She starts to unbutton her shirt.)

JACK: Yeah. Maybe you are— What about Einstein's theory of time?

ABBY: Beats me—

JACK: That time is curved.

ABBY: Yeah?

JACK: Maybe we just need to get ahead of the curve—

ABBY: Is that possible?

JACK: Why not? Did you ever think this—

(They touch: bzzzzt!)

JACK: —would be possible?

ABBY: No . . .

JACK: —Maybe it's not the end of time, but the beginning.

ABBY: Maybe it's not the last day, but the first day.

JACK: Maybe *we're* time—

ABBY: Maybe this right here— (She places his hand on the curve of her waist: crackle.) —is the curve of time—

JACK: Let's find out— (He leans into her as the wind gusts around them. Fade to black.)

END OF PLAY

Esla and Frinz
Go Partying

BRUCE SHEARER

Originally performed at Dante's in Melbourne, Australia, September 2007. Directed by the actors, with assistance from Bruce Shearer. Cast: Esla—Laura Hill; Frinz—Irene Guzowski. Also performed at Dante's, April 2008. Directed by Sean Collins. Cast: Esla—Claudia Stevens; Frinz—Fabian Lapham.

CHARACTERS

> ESLA, a cautious, careful, but enthusiastic balloon. Esla's age is flexible, from twelve up.
>
> FRINZ, a more street-smart, knowledgeable balloon. Frinz's age is flexible, from twelve up.

SETTING

> A small children's birthday party.

TIME

> The present.

. . .

Esla and Frinz, two balloons, are floating around at a noisy kids party.

ESLA: This is so wild!

FRINZ: That's the territory.

ESLA: Did you see Zento go up?

FRINZ: At least he went out with a pop.

> *(Long pause.)*

ESLA: It's not an easy business.

FRINZ: Entertainment is always precarious.

ESLA: But we're professionals.

FRINZ: *(Pause.)* Careful, watch out for the—!

ESLA: *(Gasps.)* Thanks for that, it could have been nasty.

> *(Esla and Frinz bounce around together for a few moments.)*

ESLA: Do you think it's true?

FRINZ: What?

ESLA: You know.

FRINZ: I don't.

ESLA: The story they told us about the little girl in a yellow dress who takes us home and loves us forever more.

FRINZ: It's both a matter of belief and a magical metaphor for our existence.

ESLA: But will it happen? Has it happened?

FRINZ: *(Pause.)* It could conceivably happen.

ESLA: It's got to!

FRINZ: This is your first tour of duty?

ESLA: You know it is.

FRINZ: I'll look after you.

ESLA: What about you, have you been out before?

Frinz: *(Pause.)* No, I haven't actually, but I've done a lot of reading up on it.

ESLA: Where from?

FRINZ: I've got good sources.

ESLA: You don't mean the little cardboard blurb on our packet?

FRINZ: It might be succinct, but it's very heartfelt!

ESLA: *(Quoting.)* To enhance parties, weddings, and special events, with a view to generally brightening your world.

FRINZ: That's powerful.

ESLA: But what does it really mean?

FRINZ: That we're special.

ESLA: *(Pause.)* Does it mean we have a future?

FRINZ: That's all part of the great mystery.

ESLA: You're right.

(The party noise suddenly increases.)

FRINZ: I think they're doing something.

ESLA: What?

FRINZ: The big ones are herding the little ones.

ESLA: Is that possible, they seem so fast and chaotic? I bet they bite those little ones.

FRINZ: Look, they are gathering them.

ESLA: But one is still free.

FRINZ: She's running this way.

ESLA: She's dangerous.

FRINZ: Float, Float!

ESLA: Gain altitude!

(The little girl runs through Esla and Frinz screaming at the top of her voice.)

FRINZ: Ohhh!

ESLA: Ahhh!

FRINZ: So bruising.

ESLA: A savage impact.

FRINZ: *(Long pause.)* And they call this a party.

ESLA: A party of savages.

FRINZ: We must rise above it.

ESLA: Serene.

FRINZ: Sublime.

ESLA: Offering, shape, color.

FRINZ: Festive purity, but with careful restraint.

ESLA: But do they really see us that way?

FRINZ: They should. They must!

ESLA: Or are we but playthings, to be revered admittedly, but then thrown aside like trifles.

FRINZ: *(Long pause.)* Look, that's a cake.

ESLA: Is it, how do you know?

FRINZ: It's got icing and candles.

ESLA: No.

FRINZ: Oh yes, candles, the natural predator of all balloons.

ESLA: Look they're lighting them. So beautiful! *(Esla sways toward the enticing candles.)*

FRINZ: Don't be taken in, look away from those dazzling, dancing lights!

ESLA: I can't.

FRINZ: We must resist this fatal attraction!

ESLA: But why, they're so pretty. I just want to float above them.

FRINZ: It sounds fine, but they'll lure you down to your destruction. We must be strong! *(The sound of "Happy Birthday" being sung.)*

ESLA: They are singing one of the sacred songs.

FRINZ: Oh yes they are.

ESLA: This is it.

FRINZ: The real thing.

ESLA: It's HAPPY BIRTHDAY!

> *(Esla and Frinz hug together.)*

FRINZ: I'm glad we experienced this together.

ESLA: It's the pinnacle of balloon life.

FRINZ: The party, the cake, the candles, the song!

ESLA: I want to keep this moment. I want to live like this forever.

FRINZ: Hang onto it.

ESLA: Cling to it. Let's just breathe it in for as long as we can.

FRINZ: Oh yes we must.

ESLA: *(Long pause.)* The candles are diminishing.

FRINZ: So soon they burn away.

ESLA: They're cutting the cake. But how can they? It's like shredding a dream!

FRINZ: See how the little ones devour it.

ESLA: But it's so wrong. No thanks, no appreciation of the ritual. Don't they understand what they're doing? Don't they care?

FRINZ: They experience it without comprehension.

ESLA: The moment is lost. Wasted!

> *(Esla and Frinz pause.)*

FRINZ: Oh no!

ESLA: What?

FRINZ: They're giving them the dreaded red drink.

ESLA: But surely it's been banned.

FRINZ: If only it had.

FRINZ: *(Long pause.)* They're going wild on sugar overload.

ESLA: And now the desecration comes.

> *(Esla holds Frinz tightly.)*

ESLA: But the large ones, surely they can control them.

FRINZ: Nothing can tame a little wild one on red drink. Look the big ones turn away.

ESLA: They fear to watch the beauty die.

> *(Two little children rush up and grab Esla and Frinz from behind.)*

ESLA: They've got us.

FRINZ: Don't resist, we must go with it.

ESLA: How can I?

FRINZ: Remember the code. Balloons must be smooth and relaxed at all times.

ESLA: Of course.

FRINZ: Tension makes you brittle and there lies danger.

> *(Esla is twisted and thrown around.)*

ESLA: But he's squashing me.

FRINZ: That's the territory we're in. Meditate through it. We must remember our training.

> *(Esla is bashed against the wall.)*

ESLA: He's bashing me against the wall.

FRINZ: I know, I know. You must be strong.

ESLA: Like the reed, I must bend.

FRINZ: Exactly.

> *(Esla is thrown back close to Frinz who has been serene and motionless throughout.)*

ESLA: Your little girl seems nice.

FRINZ: She's been munching on her cake.

ESLA: That seems positive.

FRINZ: But note the red-stained lips.

ESLA: Not the drink.

FRINZ: The deadly drink.

> *(Esla is squashed again as the little boy blows loud raspberries on the balloon.)*

ESLA: What an indignity.

FRINZ: Just put up with it.

ESLA: That's easy for you to say.

FRINZ: I too have my threat.

ESLA: From that quiet little girl.

FRINZ: Look down.

ESLA: Where?

FRINZ: It's in her hand.

ESLA: It's just a broach.

FRINZ: With a pin!

ESLA: She wouldn't—

FRINZ: Let's hope not.

ESLA: She's only holding it.

FRINZ: But the pin is out and it wants only one thing. To pierce the flesh of a fresh balloon.

(Esla shudders away from Frinz.)

ESLA: But she loves you. She holds you so carefully. While my oaf blurts his way through me.

FRINZ: We're expendable. We can be loved, and then lost in the same gesture.

(Esla is suddenly being flattened by the boy.)

ESLA: He's popping me.

FRINZ: No, just threatening to.

ESLA: I'm glad you can discern a difference.

FRINZ: Definitely.

(Frinz suddenly twists as the sound of a pin scraping a balloon can be heard.)

FRINZ: The pin.

ESLA: Stay still.

FRINZ: She toys with my existence.

ESLA: Hold firm, my friend.

FRINZ: The point it lusts for me.

ESLA: Resist, she may be unaware. For she smiles distractedly.

(They pause for a moment, and then Esla speaks in a dreamy tone.)

ESLA: If I'd only known it was like this. I would have happily loved the candles.

FRINZ: No.

ESLA: Even as the point searches for entry.

FRINZ: Even then.

ESLA: No, I'd rather I died in rapture with my sexy sirens as they lured me down to paradise.

FRINZ: Don't talk that way, it's against our philosophy.

ESLA: Our philosophy lies in ruins around us.

FRINZ: Yet we still survive, my friend.

ESLA: Could it be worse.

FRINZ: I fear so.

(Balloon bursting sounds.)

FRINZ: Terrible creatures.

ESLA: Look how they stamp burst and pop our brethren.

FRINZ: It can help us.

ESLA: How.

FRINZ: It distracts our tormentors momentarily.

ESLA: Yes.

FRINZ: A brief chance.

ESLA: Take it!

(Esla and Frinz start floating away.)

FRINZ: Float for the door.

ESLA: Yes, there is a breeze.

FRINZ: This is no party.

ESLA: Just carnage.

FRINZ: Quick, they gather.

ESLA: They see us.

FRINZ: They come.

ESLA: Quick.

FRINZ: We're out.

ESLA: Almost.

FRINZ: Noooo.

ESLA: Leave me, you must fly, one of us must make it.

FRINZ: I cannot leave you!

ESLA: Be quick, I'm snagged on the curtain.

FRINZ: By the sacred lips that gave us life, I will preserve your memory.

(Frinz floats free just as there is a loud pop from Esla.)

END OF PLAY

Flooding

JAMI BRANDLI

Originally produced by Moving Arts as part of
"The Car Plays" developed by Paul Nicolai Stein, artistic
producer, at the Steve Allen Theater, Hollywood, California,
October 7, 2007. Directed by Melissa Marie Thomas. Cast:
Brenda—McCready Baker; Chuck—Shaughn Bucholz.

CHARACTERS

    BRENDA, female, late twenties to early thirties, has hodophobia and can't help but check her pulse.

    CHARLE, male or female, late twenties to early thirties, has claustrophobia.

SETTING

    A car. Los Angeles.

TIME

    The present: Sunday afternoon.

• • •

Lights up. A stationary car. A Sunday afternoon in Los Angeles. Seated in the driver's seat, Brenda flips down the visor and nervously applies lip gloss. She then removes her car keys from the dash and stares at them. She can't bring herself to stick the key into the ignition. A panic attack is about to strike. Placing her fingers on her neck, she checks her pulse. A moment later, her cell phone rings. Brenda removes her fingers and scrambles to answer her phone.

BRENDA: *(Into phone.)* Hello . . . ? Jesus, Patty. You don't have to check up on me. It's been, what, five minutes since you left? I'm fine. I haven't even started your car yet. *(Goes to check pulse.)* I'm not checking my pulse. *(Takes fingers away from neck.)* Charlie isn't in the car. You think I'd be talking like this if she was? *(Goes to check pulse again.)* I'm not checking my pulse. *(Takes fingers away from neck.)* I know it brings one on if I check. My heart has a mind of its own. What do you want from me . . . ? Patty. It's not a date. Charlie and I are just going out for coffee. Like I told you. She's in my therapy group. We're doing a therapy thing called flooding. To help each other out. Like I told you. I know you support me. I know . . . Jesus. I put on some vanilla lip gloss, and you think I want to marry the woman . . . Not a date, Patty. Not. A. Date. *(Goes to check pulse again.)* I'm not checking it! *(Takes fingers away from neck.)* Jesus!
(Charlie enters stage left. She cautiously approaches the car. Brenda sees her and flips down her visor.)

BRENDA: *(Into phone.)* I'll call you later . . . Of course you're picking me up! How else am I going to get home? Drive?
(Brenda hangs up, quickly applies more lip gloss, and flips up the visor. She tries to sneak in a pulse check, but Charlie gives her a wave. She waves back

and smiles. Charlie VERY cautiously enters the car and leaves the door open.
They smile at each other. A moment.)

CHARLIE: I should close the door, shouldn't I?

BRENDA: Whenever you're ready.

(Charlie keeps the door open.)

CHARLIE: So . . .

BRENDA: Yeah?

CHARLIE: This is pretty awesome.

BRENDA: Yeah . . . Wait. What is?

CHARLIE: That you drove to my place.

BRENDA: I wish. *(Nervous laugh.)* My sister, Patty. It's her car. She drove me here. Then we called a taxi to bring her back home. So, no. Still gotta drive this baby. Still got to drive. Still got to put the key in the ignition and turn it . . .

CHARLIE: We can get coffee another time—

BRENDA: NO! I mean . . . not unless you want to get coffee another time?

CHARLIE: No. No. I definitely want to get coffee. I just have to close the door is all.

BRENDA: Right.

CHARLIE: And you have to drive to the coffee shop.

BRENDA: Right.

CHARLIE: The coffee shop is what? Like five blocks away?

BRENDA: Six.

CHARLIE: Right. That's not far.

BRENDA: Not far at all.

CHARLIE: Right . . . You know, I don't understand why people don't walk more in LA. It's only six blocks. Would it hurt us to walk there? I mean, we are killing the planet by driving.

BRENDA: Do you want to walk there?

CHARLIE: No. Do you?

BRENDA: No.

CHARLIE: That would sort of defeat the purpose.

BRENDA: Totally.

CHARLIE: We promised we would do our flooding.

BRENDA: Right.

CHARLIE: So let's do our flooding.

BRENDA: OK.

CHARLIE: Group will be pretty jealous when we tell them next week.

BRENDA: Totally.

CHARLIE: I'll just close this door.

BRENDA: And I'll put this key into the ignition.

(Charlie holds onto the door handle, and Brenda holds the car keys. They wait for the other to make a move. Neither one does. A moment.)

BRENDA: I don't like the term "flooding."

CHARLIE: Me neither.

BRENDA: It's like I have to picture myself drowning to get over my hodophobia.

CHARLIE: You have aquaphobia?

BRENDA: Oh no . . . But I am afraid of drowning.

CHARLIE: Who isn't afraid of drowning?

BRENDA: I know I am.

CHARLIE: Me, too!

BRENDA: That's so great!

CHARLIE: *(Suddenly serious.)* But I don't have aquaphobia.

BRENDA: *(Quickly.)* Me neither. *(Beat.)* I just have hodophobia.

CHARLIE: And I just have claustrophobia.

BRENDA: One phobia each.

(A moment. Charlie clutches the door handle.)

CHARLIE: Being locked in a coffin for two days can really affect you. For years.

BRENDA: Of course. I know I'd have claustrophobia AND taphephobia if I went through what you did—

CHARLIE: I don't have taphephobia—

BRENDA: Me neither. But that must have been horrific. To be locked in a coffin—by your mother of all people. I mean, how does that happen?

CHARLIE: One of the hazards of growing up in a funeral home—

BRENDA: I'd say!

CHARLIE: I was playing in the coffin and mother accidentally locked me inside. It was an accident—

BRENDA: Of course, it was an accident. Everyone in group believes you. But to feel like you're being buried alive? To not know when you were getting out? If ever? Well, that's about the worst thing I can imagine.
(Charlie's breathing has become heavy and full of panic. Brenda suddenly realizes what she's doing.)

BRENDA: Oh my God. What am I doing? I'm so sorry—I don't know why I'm bringing this up. I'm an idiot—

CHARLIE: It's okay. This is a little like flooding. You're flooding me . . . in a way . . . to make me relive the coffin . . . *(Takes in deep breath.)* I'm just going to close the door.

(She doesn't. They stare ahead. A moment. Brenda then tries to sneak a pulse check without Charlie noticing. Charlie turns to see her, and Brenda tries to cover it up by scratching her neck.)

CHARLIE: Itchy neck?

BRENDA: Yeah. Um. I mean, no. I was trying to check my pulse. It drives my sister crazy.

CHARLIE: *(Knowingly.)* Ah, yes. The uncontrollable pulse checking.

BRENDA: You have cardiophobia?

CHARLIE: Oh no. But, if I think about my heart too much, my pulse starts to race, so I have to check it.

BRENDA: Me, too!

CHARLIE: It's pretty freaky how our hearts just beat.

BRENDA: Right? I don't trust ANY involuntary muscle. I mean, the liver? What is up with that thing? And don't even get me started on the bladder.

CHARLIE: But the heart. The heart seems to have a mind of its own.

BRENDA: *(Pleasantly stunned.)* That's what I say.

CHARLIE: *(Suddenly serious.)* But I don't have cardiophobia.

BRENDA: *(Quickly.)* Me neither . . . Ready to get coffee?

CHARLIE: Absolutely.

(Charlie continues to hold the door handle and Brenda her key. A moment.)

BRENDA: I've been searching online for the term "fear of one's past," like an all Greeked-up, official term for "fear of one's past." Like pastaphobia or biographiophobia. And there isn't one. I could only find mnemophobia.

CHARLIE: You have a fear of memories?

BRENDA: Me? Oh no. At least, I don't think I do. Do you have mnemophobia?

CHARLIE: I don't think so. But . . . I do have memories.

BRENDA: Who doesn't?

CHARLIE: I mean, the coffin is a memory . . . So yeah, my memories can scare me.

BRENDA: My memories scare me, too.

CHARLIE: But I don't have mnemophobia.

BRENDA: Me neither. *(Beat.)* Except . . . Except I can't put this key into the ignition without feeling like my heart is going to explode. I get behind the wheel, and I all can do is think about is my horrible accident on the 101 from five years ago and how it was my fault—and it was my fault. I came real close to killing a bunch of people, and I don't want to kill anybody—

CHARLIE: You're not going to kill me, Brenda—

BRENDA: *(Increasing panic.)* You don't know that! I could totally kill you today! Just by driving six blocks to the coffee shop. And the accident will be caused by me because I'll be checking my pulse to make sure I'm not having a panic attack, and BAM, in a split second, I rear-end a car and a car rear-ends me and you go flying out the window and break your neck on Sunset Boulevard. And I don't want to do that to you because I haven't liked someone in a long time. I mean, really like someone. And I like you, Charlie. I really, really like you.

CHARLIE: You like me? *(A moment. Brenda's red. Charlie's smiling.)*

BRENDA: I wasn't supposed to say that out loud.

(Charlie leans over and kisses her. Brenda's tense at first, and then kisses her back. It's a great kiss.)

CHARLIE: I've wanted to do that for a long time.

BRENDA: Really?

CHARLIE: Since the first day you joined the group and I saw you checking your pulse.

BRENDA: So you knew.

CHARLIE: I think it's cute the way you try to be inconspicuous about it.

BRENDA: Thanks.

(They share a quick, soft laugh.)

CHARLIE: So this must be our first date.

BRENDA: I guess it is.

(A moment. Their confidence is building.)

CHARLIE: Brenda?

BRENDA: Yeah, Charlie?

CHARLIE: We can do our flooding.

BRENDA: We can.

CHARLIE: We have each other.

BRENDA: We do, don't we?

CHARLIE: I'm just going to close the door.

BRENDA: And I'm going to put the key into the ignition . . .

(Charlie holds onto the door handle and Brenda her key. They just can't do it. A moment.)

BRENDA: Charlie?

CHARLIE: Yeah, Brenda?

BRENDA: I was thinking that, maybe since this is our first date, that maybe we should . . . I don't know, walk to the coffee shop.

CHARLIE: I was thinking the same thing.

(Charlie and Brenda quickly get out of the car. Charlie takes Brenda's hand and they walk. Blackout.)

END OF PLAY

Fuck Tori Amos

CAITLIN MONTANYE PARRISH

Originally produced at Around the Coyote, Chicago,
February 10, 2006. Directed by Erica L. Weiss.
Cast: Audrey—Elizabeth Breen; Geoff—Walter Briggs.

CHARACTERS

AUDREY, sixteen or seventeen years old.
GEOFF, fourteen or fifteen years old.

SETTING

A living room.

TIME

The present: night time.

•   •   •

Geoff sits in the living room where a suitcase and clock also reside. After a while, his sister enters with a bottle of wine.

AUDREY: Hey.

GEOFF: Hey.

AUDREY: What are you still doing up?

GEOFF: Nothing.

AUDREY: Just hanging out?

GEOFF: You want company?

AUDREY: Sure. Thanks. How are you, little brother?

GEOFF: OK.

AUDREY: You know, just because I'm not here to argue with Dad doesn't mean I'm not shaming him wherever I am. Not that much is changing.

GEOFF: Yeah.

AUDREY: You want to get drunk?

GEOFF: No, Dad'll get pissed.

AUDREY: So what? I'm leaving in like . . . *(Looks at clock.)* Christ, it's late. Two hours. Shit, you should be in bed.

GEOFF: I'm good.

AUDREY: You want to know something useful?

GEOFF: Sure.

AUDREY: You can avoid hangovers by drinking an equal amount of water and alcohol. So drink right when you do. There's no reason to puke.

GEOFF: Dad says hangovers run in our family.

AUDREY: You should know Dad sits on a throne of lies.

GEOFF: Do you smoke pot?

AUDREY: Officially: no. Actually: oh my yes. Do you?

GEOFF: Should I?

AUDREY: Well, I waited until I was with people I knew I could trust, people with whom I knew I would have a good time, and people I knew would give me good shit. It's up to you whether you do it, but I don't think it's a big moral question. Even though if Mom asks I have NO EXPERI-ENCE WITH DRUGS WHATSOEVER.

GEOFF: Duh.

AUDREY: It's really not a big deal. Dad smoked.

GEOFF: No, he didn't.

AUDREY: He totally did.

GEOFF: When?

AUDREY: The seventies.

GEOFF: Oh.

AUDREY: He only quit because Mom made him. The zero tolerance thing is a fairly recent thing for him. Interesting how he's taken to it so thoroughly.

GEOFF: You shouldn't have let him catch you.

AUDREY: Yeah, I know.

GEOFF: Dad really used to smoke?

AUDREY: I will not swear to God, but he totally did. I found out last Christ-mas. I went to the airport to pick up Uncle Evan, who, by the way, only converted to Catholicism because he had a nervous breakdown his ju-nior year at Yale when he figured out he was gay.

GEOFF: Uncle Evan's gay?

AUDREY: Technically. He's been offering his abstinence to God as penance for a decade. That's how he could live with that fat woman for so long. Any-way, when I picked him up, we were having this really cool conversation about different things. Talking like equals, it was good. He mentioned he'd given up pot because he liked smoking in the mornings, and he couldn't do that now that he'd turned fifty. Pussy. I said I had to be care-ful smoking in the mornings because Dad was always around. And Evan said, "Yeah, Bruce hasn't smoked since he and your mom started dating." And I was like, "What?" And he was like, "Shit." It was glorious.

GEOFF: Awesome.

AUDREY: Seriously. Fuck him. Hypocrite. *(Pause.)* Thanks for staying up with me.

GEOFF: Yeah. Course.

AUDREY: You can go though, if you want.

GEOFF: It's cool.

AUDREY: I'm just gonna get trashed.

GEOFF: Go ahead.

AUDREY: I love you, man.

GEOFF: Thanks.

AUDREY: So you know, I'm glad you're my brother. Seriously. You're very cool for a younger sibling. You have a burgeoning sense of humor. You're very well kempt. You smell terrific. Congratulations.

GEOFF: I use Axe.

AUDREY: You're a cool human being is what I'm saying. Also, you should know there is no shame in an I-Love-You-Man speech. They make for excellent stories and you're usually glad you did it. I love you. Man.

GEOFF: Cool.

AUDREY: Not just as a brother, but as a person of your specific temperament. I would like you even if I didn't have to. And if there's anything I can ever help you with, like something, I will do my utmost.

GEOFF: Cool.

AUDREY: You know it, Gee-owf. *(Pause.)* So, what else? I'm packed. They're shipping me off to bad-child camp tomorrow. I have nothing but time. But time is two hours. So what else?

GEOFF: I don't know.

AUDREY: That's OK.

GEOFF: Maybe if you said you were sorry—

AUDREY: No. I'm sorry man, no. Are you going to be OK when I'm gone?

GEOFF: Dad's an asshole.

AUDREY: But you're really OK, you know? I promise. Like, there's a lot of crazy in the family, but it still works. Crazy has its own interesting little ecosystem that's self-sustaining. And it gives you better coping mechanisms. I guess.

GEOFF: I guess.

AUDREY: How would you kill somebody?

GEOFF: What?

AUDREY: Heat of passion. Or carefully planned out. How do you kill someone?

GEOFF: Knife.

AUDREY: Which?

GEOFF: Both.

AUDREY: Cool.

GEOFF: You?

AUDREY: Bludgeoning tool.

GEOFF: Nice.

AUDREY: Do you believe in God?

GEOFF: Maybe.

AUDREY: OK. That's cool. Do you remember when Dad threw away your notebook?

GEOFF: When I was ten?

AUDREY: Yeah. What the hell?

GEOFF: I don't remember.

AUDREY: That was so fucked up. What, were you writing *Mein Kampf*, or something?

GEOFF: What's *Mein Kampf*?

AUDREY: Hitler's autobiography.

GEOFF: Oh. Then, no. I really don't remember. Maybe I was drawing some weird crap or something.

AUDREY: Huh. It was weird. Hey, are you a virgin?

GEOFF: Dude.

AUDREY: Heh-heh. OK. That's cool. Do you . . . would you say you really like other people?

GEOFF: They're OK.

AUDREY: Yeah. But OK sucks. I don't like people my age. They all seem tired. It makes sense, though. High school is exhausting. People suck. What the hell, Geoff? Dad's freaking out at me because of what, exactly? I wish I could . . . I don't know. I remember in preschool there was an election between pretzels for snack time and cheese—it's for snack time. And I voted for pretzels and lost, but this other kid got a bunch of people that didn't care to vote for Cheez-its, and they won, even though pretzels are clearly the superior snack food. That's not really . . . there's something that's supposed to work in the world but it's broken. Sorry, we were talking about you.

GEOFF: No, I like pretzels.

AUDREY: Right?

GEOFF: They're really crunchy.

AUDREY: Salty crunchy.

GEOFF: Yeah, no. Talk about what you want.

AUDREY: Thanks. Never let people fuck you around. Never let Dad win just 'cause he's louder. And never. Never ever let a girl convince you that you, for any reason, ever have to listen to Tori Amos. If she says you'll like it, she's a filthy little bitch whore of a liar. The day I realized all good had been sucked from music was the day I heard her cover of "Smells Like Teen Spirit." Something in me shriveled and died that I can never get back. It's like a little raisin that lives in my lungs. Ooh, look at me. I play piano and have red hair. I was raped. I must be talented.

GEOFF: Maybe you should try to get some sleep.

AUDREY: No, I can't sleep. Kurt Cobain would roll over in his heroin-soaked grave if he heard that submissive bitch of a cover. Kurt was very sensitive. Typical Pisces.

GEOFF: Like you.

AUDREY: I guess. I'm cusp of Aries, and Aries don't believe in astrology. But yeah, typical Pisces.

GEOFF: I was sitting downstairs. And it was like, "Audrey's leaving." I'm not the good kid if I'm the only kid. Right? That doesn't work, I don't think. And then I thought, "How come I'm the good one?" I don't know. You're really cool. I'm glad you're my sister. I'm glad that if I have kids, you'll be their aunt. So don't, while you're away, like, think I don't miss you. This sucks. Is it OK if I'm here until you go?

AUDREY: Please.

GEOFF: Cool. I love you, man. Audrey.

AUDREY: Yeah, Geoff. Definitely. So. What have you learned?

GEOFF: Water equals no hangovers. Dad has done drugs. Gay uncle. People bad. Pretzels good. Fuck Tori Amos.

AUDREY: Fuck Tori Amos. Are you sure you don't want some?

GEOFF: Yeah, OK.

AUDREY: Sweet. Do you know about condoms?

END OF PLAY

A Funeral Home in Brooklyn

DAVID JOHNSTON

Originally produced by Blue Coyote Theater Group at the
Access Theater, New York City, as part of The Standards of
Decency Project, December 12–17, 2006 and January 3–8,
2007. Directed by Kyle Ancowitz. Cast: Man—
Robert Buckwalter; Woman—Tracey Gilbert.

MAN, late thirties, early forties.

WOMAN, early to midthirties, working class.

SETTING

A small nondescript office, a desk and a chair.

TIME

The present.

· · ·

Lights up. The man is seated behind the desk. He is somberly dressed in a dark suit. The Woman is seated in a chair, her purse on the floor. Her eyes are red from crying. She occasionally dabs at her eyes with a handkerchief.

WOMAN: Thank you for seeing me.

MAN: Of course. It's a difficult time.

WOMAN: Yes. It is.

MAN: And we're very sorry for your loss.

WOMAN: Thank you.

MAN: You were close?

WOMAN: Yes. Daddy was a wonderful man.

MAN: And it was so sudden.

WOMAN: We just had Sunday dinner together a few days ago. Mom, Daddy, all the grandkids. Me and my brother. Just like usual. He seemed fine.

MAN: I'm so sorry.

WOMAN: He was worried about the Mets. Hogging the remote. Nothing out of the ordinary. Then. This morning. His heart.

MAN: Yes.

WOMAN: Excuse me. I'm very upset.

MAN: Whatever we can do to help.

WOMAN: Thank you.

MAN: That's what we're here for.

(Pause.)

WOMAN: I just have to ask you. Nothing has been—done—to the body yet, has it?

MAN: If you mean embalming—

(Woman shudders.)

MAN: I'm sorry—no—no—nothing has happened. The deceased arrived here—less than an hour ago.

WOMAN: Thank goodness.

MAN: We got the call, picked him up about an hour ago—

WOMAN: I was in Bensonhurst, I drove over as soon as my brother called—

MAN: Your sister-in-law indicated cremation—

(Woman puts her face in her hands.)

MAN: I'm sorry, this is upsetting for you, we can discuss these things—

WOMAN: Cremation. Oh. No. *(She pauses, takes a few breaths.)* I—my family—we all feel that cremation—is out of the question. It's barbaric. It's not done. My sister-in-law has a habit of . . . making decisions that are not her business. My family has a certain way of doing things. We have always done things a certain way. And sometimes my sister-in-law doesn't approve. But I never thought she would go so far as to try and have him cremated before we could stop her.

MAN: Nothing has been done yet.

WOMAN: I'm so relieved I got here in time.

MAN: No decisions have been made.

WOMAN: So I can take Daddy.

(Pause.)

MAN: Well. Of course. If that is the family's wish. If the family wants another funeral home to—

WOMAN: I'm not taking him to another funeral home. I'm taking Daddy home. To Coney Island. My mother's waiting. My whole family's waiting. I have a car service outside. If someone could help—me with him—then I can take it from there.

MAN: I'm not sure I understand.

WOMAN: I'm sorry for the inconvenience.

MAN: You want to take him to another funeral home in Coney Island?

WOMAN: No, I'm sorry, I'm not being clear. I want to take him home home. Back to the apartment. In Coney Island.

MAN: Why do you want to take him home before he's been embalmed?

(Pause.)

WOMAN: So that we can eat him. *(Pause.)* Obviously. *(Pause.)* You look confused, let me explain my family. We're originally Phoenician but we settled in Egypt—oh—three thousand years ago. There's some Assyrian and Lydian in the family tree—there's always an Assyrian in the woodpile, as my grandmother used to say. But basically we're just good Phoenician stock. After the war, my grandparents moved to Coney Island. We've been in Brooklyn ever since. We're very traditional, we still follow the ancient gods. Since we believe the earth is a god—a living thing—we don't bury our dead. You don't feed a god a dead thing. Same thing with fire—fire is a god, you don't give a god a dead thing, so no cremation. It would be—to us—blasphemy. So for generations since—oh I don't know—800 BC—when our loved ones pass away, we eat them. That way, they're always a part of us. They're with us. There's continuity. It's comforting. It's an old ritual and I'm sure it seems odd to some people, but I don't understand why Orthodox Jews can't use the elevator on Saturday, so there you go.

(*Pause.*)

MAN: You want to what?

WOMAN: I'm sorry?

MAN: You want to—do what now?

WOMAN: (*As if to a none-too-bright child.*) I want to take my father's body. I have a car service outside waiting. The meter is running. I'm taking him back to Coney Island. Then we eat him.

MAN: Eat him.

WOMAN: And after that, I'm going to have a talk with my brother about his wife.

MAN: You want to—

WOMAN: She has really crossed the line this time.

MAN: Is this a joke?

WOMAN: I can assure you there is nothing funny about eating my father.

MAN: This has got to be a joke.

WOMAN: We grieve, we say good-bye, we eat.

MAN: I'm going to throw up.

WOMAN: Are you all right? I have Tums.

MAN: That's the most disgusting thing I've ever heard in my life! Get out of here before I start throwing up!

(*Pause.*)

WOMAN: I think I'd like to speak to another customer service representative.

MAN: What?

WOMAN: Someone a little more sensitive to the grieving process.

MAN: The grieving—

WOMAN: The owner. I'd like to speak to the owner.

MAN: I am the owner, lady, and I am not giving you your father's dead body to eat!

WOMAN: What is the problem here? What exactly is the problem? I grew up in Coney Island. I live in Canarsie. My father is dead. He loved the Mets and repaired watches. My mother is a retired nursing home administrator. I have a husband and two kids. I work in accounts receivable for ConEd. We're part Irish, and my family worships ancient Phoenician gods. We occasionally attend a Presbyterian church and we eat our dead. Now what exactly is the problem?

MAN: Get out of here.

WOMAN: I will go to the state attorney general's office.

MAN: And say what?

WOMAN: That this funeral home has taken my father's body and refused to give it back.

MAN: So you can eat him.

WOMAN: Yes, so we can eat him.

MAN: And what do you think the state attorney general's office is going to say?

WOMAN: Well I would hope that after twelve years of George Pataki they would be a little more responsive to the needs of middle-class New Yorkers.

MAN: This is crazy. You're crazy.

WOMAN: I don't know why you're behaving this way. It's not like I'm saying you have to eat him.

MAN: Lady, you can't eat a dead body.

WOMAN: My grandparents ate their parents. My parents ate my grandparents. I fully intend to eat both of my parents. I'm just eating Daddy first. And when my children are grown, and married, and have kids of their own, and I'm gone, they can eat me.

MAN: For one thing—

WOMAN: Some eat their dead, some bury them in Staten Island. Different strokes.

MAN: For one thing, you'll poison yourself.

WOMAN: Not unless some idiot embalms him.

MAN: It doesn't matter if he's embalmed! You can't eat dead people! It's disgusting! They're rotten! You'll die!

WOMAN: We have a stove, you know. We have kosher salt.

MAN: This is—

WOMAN: It's not like we're poor.

MAN: Get out.

WOMAN: What?

MAN: Get out before I call the cops.

WOMAN: I would have thought a funeral home in Brooklyn would have a little more respect for diversity.

MAN: Get out.

WOMAN: I don't know how you expect to stay in business.

(Man picks up a phone on the desk and starts dialing.)

WOMAN: OK, Mr. Hardball. *(She opens her purse. He flinches. She pulls out an envelope and holds it out.)* Count it.

(He hesitates.)

WOMAN: I didn't just fall off the trireme from Phoenicia, pal.

(He takes the envelope, puts down the phone, and counts the bills inside. She watches.)

MAN: All this?

WOMAN: All that. Then I take Daddy, put him in the car, take him to Coney Island.

MAN: Shut up.

WOMAN: I need the good Pyrex baking dish, the meat thermometer, the chainsaw . . .

MAN: I DON'T WANNA HEAR IT!

(He puts the envelope in his pocket.)

WOMAN: Well. I think we're done here.

(She takes her purse, gets up to leave.)

MAN: Get out and don't ever let me see you again.

WOMAN: Oh don't you worry about that.

MAN: Never.

WOMAN: And don't expect a recommendation.

MAN: OUT!

WOMAN: I'll tell my friends to go to a funeral home where family traditions are respected!

(Blackout.)

END OF PLAY

Godfrey

IAN AUGUST

Originally produced by the Native Aliens Theatre Collective,
as part of Short Stories 8: Urban Views at the
independent! theater, New York City, June 19–23, 2007.
Directed by Liza Ramirez. Cast: Helen—Jennifer Cintron;
Godfrey—Jess Cassidy White.

Thanks to Nancy Rogers and Native Aliens, Liza Ramirez,
Sue Yacka and Jillian Garai, and my Emcee.

CHARACTERS

> GODFREY, late twenties, early thirties.
> HELEN, the tooth fairy.

SETTING

> New York City, downtown, curbside.

TIME

> The present.

. . .

*Lights up. Godfrey is on the ground, slumped over in a pool of blood. His
face is bloody, as are his clothes. Helen enters, dusting off her pants, a huge
purse slung around her shoulder. She looks around and sees him.*

HELEN: I'm here! I'm here! Forty-five minutes up to my wings in traffic on the
Van Wyck, but I'm here! Well, aren't you going to say anything? Helloooo?
This *is* the right place, huh? Jeezus, if I got the wrong address—I said to
Raphael to get a new answering machine. Ours spits at you—goes *(She
makes fizzy noises.),* you can't hear a damn thing, but I was saving up for
a . . .

> *(Godfrey gets to his hands and knees; he holds his face with one hand.)*

HELEN: Woof. Are you OK?

GODFREY: *(Coughing.)* What does it look like?

HELEN: It looks like you got the crap kicked out of you. Oh, jeez, don't bleed
on my shoes. They're brand new. I practically ripped incisors out of ten-
year-olds for these shoes. Capezios. Not cheap, bucko. Oh my God, you're
really . . . huh. Drippy. Wait, I may have—I think I have a towel. Hold
on . . .

GODFREY: Oh, my nose. I think they broke my nose . . .

HELEN: It's not broken . . . you sure are, that's a lotta blood, wow! *(She hands
him the towel.)* Hold this to your nose and press the bridge. Do *not* lean
backwards. I know they tell you to lean backwards, but it's a myth—you'll
swallow the blood and you can choke. Sit up—here—

GODFREY: Ow ow ow ow ow—careful where you—

HELEN: Your ribs? Oh . . . I'm sorry.

GODFREY: Just—just let me sit here for a minute. Just back away for a minute.

HELEN: I was just—

GODFREY: A minute—

HELEN: Well if you—

GODFREY: Please!

HELEN: Fine.

GODFREY: Fine?

HELEN: Yeah, fine. I have work to do anyway.

(She puts on rubber gloves, begins to crawl around on her hands and knees, searching for something.)

GODFREY: What . . . what are you doing?

HELEN: What does it look like I'm doing? *(She crawls to him.)* Open your mouth.

GODFREY: Oh my God, they knocked out a tooth . . . I can feel the hole in my—

HELEN: Open your mouth. Lemme see. *(He does so.)* Uh-huh. Third molar from the back, top left side. *(Peering more closely.)* D two E dash seven A. OK. Close it up, Bucko.

GODFREY: I can't believe they . . . my mother's going have a fit.

HELEN: *(Resuming her search.)* So's your dentist.

GODFREY: They just jumped me . . . out of the blue. One of them had a Raiders jacket on. I don't even know what sport that is. I should call the cops. I should call an ambulance. What are you looking for?

HELEN: You bleed a lot. I can't find anything in this. It's like soup. It's like searching for a pine nut in split pea.

GODFREY: What?

HELEN: It's an expression. *(She exhales dramatically.)* All right, I give up. *(She moves to him.)* I'm gonna have a smoke. Do you mind if I smoke?

GODFREY: Who are you?

HELEN: Helen. You don't have a light, do you?

GODFREY: Of course. I keep matches up my bloody nose.

HELEN: You'll be fine. Just hold the towel—don't look at it—just hold the towel up there. I've had to do this a billion times before. My husband, Rafael, chronic nose bleeds. I mean, once or twice a year, allergies or something, and BAM! It's like a pipe bursts; the man just can't stop. I scream "Rafael! If you come near me with that leaky schnoz I'll take you out in the back-yard and stick a rock in your eye!," and I chase him with an egg beater until the bastard goes and sits in the bathtub. I made up my mind thirty years ago—if he's gonna drip blood all over my linoleum, he better be dying.

GODFREY: I'm dying.

HELEN: You're not dying.

GODFREY: I wish I were dying.

HELEN: Get over yourself. Look—Stopping.

GODFREY: Yeah.

HELEN: Thank God.

GODFREY: I'd rather not.

HELEN: Well then, thank Rafael. It's his towel. You can keep it.

GODFREY: Look . . . Helen—

HELEN: Take the towel down. Take it down from your face and lemme see. See now? It stopped. I'm gonna be gentle and wipe some of this—stop wincing, you baby. You've got broken ribs—you can handle a little dabbing. *(She wipes his face.)* Hello? Fella? Are you there under all that goop? Who is it? *(Taking the towel away.)* Hey, you're a not a bad-looking little guy.

GODFREY: Thank you.

HELEN: *(She resumes wiping.)* What's your name, kiddo?

GODFREY: Godfrey.

HELEN: And what do you do, Godfrey?

GODFREY: I'm a divorce attorney.

HELEN: Really? I'm surprised.

GODFREY: Why—the Burberry?

HELEN: I hate Burberry.

GODFREY: I hate taffeta.

HELEN: And what, pray tell, did you do to deserve this special treatment?

GODFREY: Wrong place at the wrong time . . . Some drunken assholes started chasing me.

HELEN: Assholes often have good sneakers.

GODFREY: One of them had a chunk of concrete.

HELEN: On his feet?

GODFREY: In his hand.

HELEN: That explains a lot. *(Looking at the blood-soaked towel.)* This isn't working anymore. We're saturated. Like Rafael after a margarita bender. Lemme see if I have a handi-wipey thing. *(Rummaging through her bag.)*

GODFREY: I just couldn't run fast enough.

HELEN: I think I do. I've got everything in here but a damn match.

GODFREY: I wish I'd kept that Bally's membership.

HELEN: Those things are overpriced. Ah! Here we go. *(She pulls it out.)* And it's a *disinfecting* wipey thing. You'll smell like a clean toilet, but it'll get some of the dirt out of your puffy eye.

GODFREY: They saw me coming out of a club on Christopher Street.

HELEN: What were you doing on Christopher Street?

GODFREY: Guess.

HELEN: And what were *they* doing on Christopher Street?

GODFREY: All that running made it pretty tough to play twenty questions— Ow! Stings!

HELEN: I just mean, you'd think a person of your . . . preference, persuasion, proclivity, whatever . . . doesn't have to worry on Christopher Street.

GODFREY: I guess we do.

HELEN: A gay divorce lawyer. There's something ironic in that.

GODFREY: Yet oddly satisfying.

HELEN: I just hate incidents like this. It's sinister, you know? Gives me the willies.

GODFREY: It's the nature of mankind.

HELEN: That's pretty cynical for a guy in Burberry.

GODFREY: Society's gone to shit. These guys were just the ones that got me.

HELEN: That's a little morbid.

GODFREY: I think I have the right. Look around you—I mean, *really* look: This country is filled with people so ignorant and intolerant that they'd sooner carve up their own children than compromise. You see it every day: obnoxious, bombastic morons acting out of animalistic greed and pride. Read the paper, Helen—a woman pushes her son into a twenty-foot well—a man beats his wife to death with a metal pipe and then shoots a neighbor who comes to her aid—

HELEN: I read that—that was terrible.

GODFREY: These aren't isolated incidents. These things happen every day, and we only hear about how many? Half of them? A third? Children shooting themselves in schools, drunk idiots plowing down entire families with SUVs. Today . . . it was just my turn. Had to happen sooner or later.

HELEN: That . . . sounds like a crock of defeatist bullshit, Godfrey.

GODFREY: I'm not saying that there aren't good people out there—There are. You, for example. A kind, generous woman—what is it you do, Helen?

HELEN: I'm the tooth fairy.

GODFREY: You're a fairy?

HELEN: Yeah.

GODFREY: Me too.

HELEN: You don't believe me.

GODFREY: Doesn't matter. What I'm saying is that you're probably one of the only good . . . tooth fairies . . . out there. You know? The odds weren't in my favor that you would be the one to come along to find me.

HELEN: Actually, they were pretty strong. I'm the only tooth fairy. You lost a tooth.

GODFREY: Not a good example then. OK, say you were a tennis pro—

HELEN: I understand you, Godfrey, I just don't agree. You can't live your life thinking that the whole world has gone to hell, you know?

GODFREY: No matter how I live my life, that's not going to change. Nothing I can do will change that. It's just the way it is. I've accepted it.

HELEN: You're single, huh?

GODFREY: What does that have to—

HELEN: You don't have a . . . what would you call—a boyfriend? Partner? Husband? Can you say husband if you're not in Massachusetts or Canada?

GODFREY: No, I—

HELEN: Significant other? Although that term begs the question, does one have an insignificant other as well? Is it your husband on one side and your goldfish on the other?

GODFREY: I don't—

HELEN: Although, sometimes I like my goldfish more than my husband. Blinky. Very dependable. Get a pet, Godfrey. You'd like a pet.

GODFREY: What does that have to—

HELEN: It's easy to hate the world when you don't have anyone to share it with. Attila the Hun was like that.

GODFREY: Attila the Hun?

HELEN: I've been around for a while, Godfrey. I'm the tooth fairy. You need to date more. Are you dating?

GODFREY: I'm not taking romantic advice from a woman who thinks she's the tooth fairy.

HELEN: Even though I'm the *good* tooth fairy?

GODFREY: You're mocking me.

HELEN: A little. But you need to lighten up, kiddo. Well, maybe not today. You earned a little anger today. But tomorrow you need to look out and pick up whatever pieces are laying beside you on the floor and put them back together. Trust me—there's as much good out there as there is evil. And I should know. I've been around for a couple of millennia, you know? For every Hitler there's a Mother Theresa.

GODFREY: For every Stalin?

HELEN: There's a Gandhi.

GODFREY: Mussolini.

HELEN: Abraham Lincoln!

GODFREY: Jeffrey Dahmer!

HELEN: Angela Lansbury!

GODFREY: Angela Lansbury?

HELEN: Come on—that one should speak for itself.

GODFREY: Oh, puh-lease.

HELEN: We're all of us people. Godfrey. Nelson Mandela *and* Sharon Stone. We've all lost a few teeth along the way. It's the great equalizer. Take it from me—all mouths work the same. *(She pauses, looking down.)* Oh! Lookie here!

GODFREY: What?

HELEN: Found it. D two E dash seven A. Good. *(She stands.)* Look, I've got to get back to the office. I'll call you an ambulance or something. Oh, yeah—I almost forgot. This is for you.

GODFREY: A quarter?

HELEN: This economy sucks. Take what you can get.

GODFREY: Sure.

HELEN: Don't look so down, sweetie. As if the only thing you got today was a beating and a quarter? Come on—you got to meet the tooth fairy. Give us a smile, honey—give Momma a little smile. *(Godfrey smiles.)* There we go. What a looker you are. You won't have any trouble finding a significant other. Even if he is a goldfish.

GODFREY: Thank you, Helen.

HELEN: I've got to be in Peru in an hour. Heal quickly. I'm not sending Santa over to cart your lazy ass around. *(She blows a kiss.)* Ta!

(Helen exits. Godfrey sits, looking after her. He holds up his quarter, places it in his pocket, and waits for the ambulance to arrive. Lights fade to black.)

END OF PLAY

A Great-Looking Boat

JOAN ACKERMANN

Originally performed at Mixed Company Theatre,
Great Barrington, Massachusetts, 2006.
Directed by Gillian Seidl. Cast: Elaine Fink—
Joan Ackermann; Mr. Caragianis—George Bergen.

CHARACTERS

ELAINE FINK, a woman in her late thirties or forties who marches to the beat of her own drum. In this scene, she has made an effort to dress up a little but has not completely succeeded. She might wear some unusual or bold piece of jewelry or clothing; perhaps an odd hat or high-heeled boots.

MR. CARAGIANIS, a blind, erudite older gentleman, any age over fifty, who lives alone. His clothes and furnishings reflect practicality and a simple elegance rather than wealth.

SETTING

Living room of an older scholarly gentleman. Just a few pieces of furniture will suffice. A small couch, or divan with a standing lamp nearby. A small table with a book on it. One chair.

TIME

The present.

•   •   •

At the top of the scene, gentle snoring is heard in pitch-black darkness. There's a knock on the door, which has been left slightly ajar for a visitor.

ELAINE: *(Calling in, tentatively.)* Hello. *(No response.)* Hel-looo. Ooo-ooo. Mr. Caragianis?

MR. CARAGIANIS: *(Stirring.)* Who is it?

ELAINE: Elaine Fink. *(She clears her throat.)* I'm here to read to you.

MR. CARAGIANIS: Come in. Come in.

(Pause.)

ELAINE: It's a little dark in here.

MR. CARAGIANIS: The light's in the corner.

(There's a small crash as Elaine enters in the dark, bumping into something.)

ELAINE: Which corner?

MR. CARAGIANIS: Where's Stewart?

ELAINE: Stewart couldn't come today. He had a family obligation. I'm filling in for him. *(Pause.)* Do you want me to go?

MR. CARAGIANIS: You haven't read to me yet.

(Silence.)

MR. CARAGIANIS: Are you a good reader?

ELAINE: *(Tentatively.)* Yes.

MR. CARAGIANIS: I'll be the judge of that.

> *(The lights come up revealing Mr. Caragianis, who is turning on a lamp. Elaine, clutching a small pastry box, stares at him, riveted. Frozen. He makes his way back to the couch.)*

ELAINE: I'm sorry I'm late. I had a few—unforeseen—mishaps.

> *(He doesn't respond. She stands there somewhat stiffly, unsure.)*

ELAINE: Stewart said you're reading *The Odyssey.*

MR. CARAGIANIS: You can pull up that chair.

> *(He sits on the couch, perhaps lying back against embroidered cushions, as Elaine brings the chair over to the foot of the couch.)*

MR. CARAGIANIS: The book's on the table.

> *(She goes over and gets the book off the small table near the door, depositing the pastry box on the table. She comes back, sits in the chair, and takes out a bookmark marking a place in the text.)*

ELAINE: So—

MR. CARAGIANIS: You're planning to read to my feet?

> *(Elaine looks at him; at his feet. Picks up the chair and the book and brings them around to the other end, closer to where his head rests up against cushions.)*

MR. CARAGIANIS: Do you want some juice? Apple juice?

ELAINE: No.

MR. CARAGIANIS: Stewart likes apple juice.

> *(Pause.)*

ELAINE: Should I start?

MR. CARAGIANIS: What are you waiting for?

ELAINE: OK. Page eighty-nine— *(Not sure where.)* Um . . .

> *(Mr. Caragianis. quotes, quite beautifully—)*

MR. CARAGIANIS: Skheria then came slowly into view
Like a rough shield of bull's hide on the sea.

> *(Elaine, slightly intimidated, starts reading at a brisk clip with no color at all.)*

ELAINE: But now the god of earthquake, storming home
Over the mountains of Asia from the sunburned land,
Sighted him far away. The god grew sullen
And tossed his great head, muttering to himself.

MR. CARAGIANIS: Slow down.

ELAINE: What?

MR. CARAGIANIS: Slow down. You're in overdrive.

> *(Growing more self-conscious, she slows down but reads very quietly.)*

ELAINE: Here is a pretty cruise! While I was gone

The gods have changed their minds about Odysseus.
Look at him now, just offshore of that island
That frees him from the bondage of his exile!
Still I can give him a rough ride in, and will.

MR. CARAGIANIS: Louder.

ELAINE: Brewing high thunderheads, he churned the deep
With both hands on his trident—called up wind
From every quarter, and sent a wall of rain
To blot out land and wine-dark sea in torrential night.

MR. CARAGIANIS: Louder!

(She increases her volume and starts to speed up again as she becomes increasingly more insecure.)

ELAINE: Hurricane winds now struck from the south and east
Shifting northwest in a great spume of seas,
On which Odysseus's knees grew slack, his heart
Sickened, and he said within himself:

MR. CARAGIANIS: *(Groaning.)* Unh.

(She glances over at him and comes close to yelling, not hearing him asking her to stop.)

ELAINE: "Rag of man that I am, is this the end of me?"
A great wave drove at him with toppling crest
Spinning him round, in one tremendous blow,
And he went plunging overboard, the oar haft

MR. CARAGIANIS: Stop.

ELAINE: Wrenched from his grip. A gust that came on howling
At the same instant broke his mast in two,
Across the foaming water, to and fro,
The boat careered like a ball of tumbleweed.

MR. CARAGIANIS: Stop!

(Elaine stops; looks over at him, startled.)

MR. CARAGIANIS: I can't understand a word you're saying.

(Silence.)

ELAINE: *(Irked.)* I'm reading.

MR. CARAGIANIS: Reading? You sound like you're shelling peas in your mouth with an ill-fitting pair of dentures. And pelting them across the room. You need to enunciate, clearly. It's garble—all garble. You're mangling the text.

(He shakes his head and she looks away.)

MR. CARAGIANIS: Are you familiar with *The Odyssey*?

ELAINE: *(Wary, defensive.)* Yes.

MR. CARAGIANIS: You've read it?

ELAINE: No. Maybe. In college, I might have.

MR. CARAGIANIS: You're a college graduate?

ELAINE: Yes. I have a BA. Bachelor of arts.

> *(Silence.)*

MR. CARAGIANIS: What do you like to read, Elaine?

ELAINE: *(Shrugging.)* I don't know.

MR. CARAGIANIS: *(Lamenting his absence.)* Stewart. Stewart. Stewart. Where are you?

> *(Elaine resumes reading, slowly. Enunciating aggressively, hitting every vowel and consonant overly clearly with a simmering anger.)*

ELAINE: Now the big wave a long time kept him under,

> Helpless to surface, held by tons of water,
>
> Tangled, too, by the sea cloak of Kalypso.
>
> Long, long, until he came up sprouting
>
> But still bethought him, half-drowned as he was,
>
> To flounder for the boat and get a handhold
>
> Into the bilge—to crouch there, foiling death.

MR. CARAGIANIS: Let me ask you a question, Elaine. Why are you here?

ELAINE: *(Defensively.)* I read that well.

MR. CARAGIANIS: Why . . . are you here?

ELAINE: To read to you.

MR. CARAGIANIS: I know that. But why?

> *(She tries to come up with the right answer.)*

ELAINE: Contribute.

MR. CARAGIANIS: Contribute to what?

> *(Again, she struggles for an answer.)*

ELAINE: *(Mumbling.)* Humanity.

MR. CARAGIANIS: What? What did you say?

ELAINE: Humanity!

MR. CARAGIANIS: *(Pondering.)* Humanity—

ELAINE: For soul. Enrichment.

MR. CARAGIANIS: Whose soul are you hoping to enrich? Yours or mine?

> *(She doesn't answer.)*

MR. CARAGIANIS: Tell me—how do you usually spend your Saturday afternoons, Elaine? When you're not reading to an old blind man? *(No response.)* Hello?

ELAINE: I used to volunteer at the food pantry.

MR. CARAGIANIS: Ahhh. So Saturday afternoons are for noble causes. Contributing to humanity, cultivating the tender sprouts of your munificence to shower goodwill and benevolence upon the needy, the poor, the infirm. Well, isn't the food pantry missing you there today?

ELAINE: They kicked me out.

MR. CARAGIANIS: The food pantry kicked you out? What on earth for? *(Silence.)* You must have done something very wicked.

ELAINE: I got into a fight.

MR. CARAGIANIS: Good God. A fist fight?

ELAINE: No. Some woman wanted a third frozen chicken.

MR. CARAGIANIS: A frozen chicken. Was that so unreasonable?

ELAINE: She already had two. I wasn't about to give her a third.

MR. CARAGIANIS: And?

ELAINE: She threw one at me.

MR. CARAGIANIS: She threw a frozen chicken at you?

ELAINE: At my head. I threw it right back. Took her right down.

(He takes in this information. Reassesses.)

MR. CARAGIANIS: Are you married, Elaine?

ELAINE: No.

MR. CARAGIANIS: Divorced?

ELAINE: I wish.

MR. CARAGIANIS: You wish you were divorced?

ELAINE: I've always wanted to be divorced.

MR. CARAGIANIS: Why?

ELAINE: It just—connotes—so much history. Without the hassle of being married. *(Silence.)* Do you want me to keep reading?

MR. CARAGIANIS: I'm not sure.

ELAINE: *(Checking her watch.)* My ride doesn't get here for another forty-five minutes.

MR. CARAGIANIS: You're not possessed of your own automobile?

ELAINE: No.

MR. CARAGIANIS: Judging from a small but telling smattering of details, Elaine, I would say that your life is lacking in several departments.

(She takes offense but doesn't respond, brooding. He gets up and begins to move around.)

MR. CARAGIANIS: Well, since we have forty-five minutes to share, perhaps you'd be interested in hearing why the epic poet Homer is considered one of the greatest imaginations in Western civilization? *(No response.)* Well?

ELAINE: *(Watching him move.)* Can I just ask you a question?

MR. CARAGIANIS: Fire away.

ELAINE: Were you born blind?

MR. CARAGIANIS: Yes.

ELAINE: You were born blind; you didn't become blind.

MR. CARAGIANIS: That's correct.

ELAINE: You've never been able to see?

MR. CARAGIANIS: Correct.

ELAINE: Can I just ask you another question?

MR. CARAGIANIS: Go ahead. You're on a roll.

ELAINE: When someone reads to you about boats out on the wine-dark sea, what do you see? In your mind? If you've never seen a boat, how can you imagine one?

MR. CARAGIANIS: Very easily.

ELAINE: *(Genuinely curious.)* But, how can you imagine something you've never seen? You've never seen the ocean, how can you begin to picture big . . . gigantic . . . foamy waves . . . with a boat tossed around on top?

MR. CARAGIANIS: Well— What is a boat? A vessel that carries people on the water. I can imagine that.

ELAINE: What if you were way off?

MR. CARAGIANIS: Maybe what I see in my mind's eye is far more fabulous. More astonishing.

(Elaine ponders, staring at him.)

ELAINE: I wish I could see . . . the boat in your mind. Out on the ocean. *(She laughs to herself.)* That's gotta be wild.

(He takes mild umbrage at this.)

MR. CARAGIANIS: Just out of curiosity, Elaine . . . What is your last name?

ELAINE: Fink.

MR. CARAGIANIS: Fink. Mm. No, I'm just interested to know . . . My limited imagination has—all the while we've been sitting here, conversing, sharing, getting acquainted—been busy, at work constructing, "imagining" exactly what the circumstances might have been surrounding your tardy arrival today.

ELAINE: Huh?

(He approaches her from behind, increasingly bearing down on her.)

MR. CARAGIANIS: You said you were late . . . due to unforeseen mishaps. I can't help but wonder—based on intuition and the voluminous amounts of unsolicited information you have imparted to me. On reflection, would you say, Elaine, that any of those "mishaps" were actually, in fact, premeditated? Possibly of your own unconscious making? And did any of them involve . . . loss? Fear? Disappointment? Or, deep repressed rage? *(After a couple of moments, her anger kicks in.)*

ELAINE: *(Standing.)* Look, Mr. Caragianis. You may have a great-looking boat in your mind, but you have absolutely no clear picture of me. *(After gathering her things and heading for the door, she turns back.)* And—it doesn't take a genius to see that my life is lacking in several departments. Furthermore—someone once told me that I am an excellent reader and that my reading voice is extremely pleasant and even actually mellifluous.

MR. CARAGIANIS: Ha! Who told you that?

ELAINE: *(Gloating.)* Stewart!

MR. CARAGIANIS: Stewart?

ELAINE: Yes, Stewart, your favorite. Stewart who likes apple juice, who is off at a family obligation—namely, marrying some telecommunications woman he hardly knows, who he knocked up last summer in Montreal when he lied to me about being in Boise, Idaho, visiting a dying uncle. And . . . who lied to me repeatedly about being here, reading to you, when he was busy doing I don't even know what with I don't even know who, but you can be sure he didn't have his clothes on while he was doing it. And yes . . . being on the phone with Stewart is what made me late and yes—loss. Fear. Rage. Sure, all of the above!

(Tearful and upset, she reaches for the pastry box, yanks off the string, and takes out a large chocolate-covered cream puff. Aggressively, she sinks her teeth into it, drowning her sorrows in it. After a while, he asks:)

MR. CARAGIANIS: What are you eating?

ELAINE: *(Pissed off, mouth full.)* A cream puff.

MR. CARAGIANIS: Cream puff?

ELAINE: I brought you one. *(Sarcastically.)* To enrich my soul.

MR. CARAGIANIS: I'll take it.

(He extends his hand. After a moment, she reaches down and lifts one out of the box for him. Hands it to him on a napkin and watches as he smells and examines it with his fingers. They both eat in silence for a moment.)

MR. CARAGIANIS: I haven't had a cream puff for decades.

(They keep eating. Still holding the cream puff, which is quite messy, Elaine picks up the book, sits down on the couch, initially with her back to him, and resumes reading.)

ELAINE: But Ino saw him—Ino, Kadmos's daughter,
Slim-legged, lovely, once an earthling girl.

MR. CARAGIANIS: *(Grimacing slightly.)* Forget it. You don't have to read.

ELAINE: I want to.

MR. CARAGIANIS: Why?

ELAINE: *(She turns and looks at him.)* I want to know what happens.

> *(After her emotional outburst, she now reads calmly, resigned, not caring how she sounds; a simple, direct delivery. The words and story seem to hold a special significance for her. Still consuming large bites.)*

ELAINE: Touched by Odysseus's painful buffeting

> She broke the surface, like a diving bird,
>
> To rest upon the tossing raft and say:
>
> "O forlorn man, I wonder
>
> Why the Earthshaker, Lord Poseidon, holds
>
> This fearful grudge—father of all your woes.
>
> He will not drown you, though, despite his rage.
>
> You seem clear-headed still; do what I tell you.
>
> Shed that cloak, let the gale take your craft,
>
> And swim for it—swim hard to get ashore
>
> Upon Skheria—

MR. CARAGIANIS: *(Correcting her pronunciation.)* Skheria.

> *(Mildly annoyed, she continues.)*

ELAINE: . . . yonder, Where it is fated that you find a shelter.

MR. CARAGIANIS: My God—

ELAINE: You're interrupting. Please stop interrupting.

MR. CARAGIANIS: I'm sorry. *(Tickled, delighted.)* It's just—this is so good! Delicious! I'd forgotten cream puffs even existed.

> *(She stares at him, sitting next to her. He is absolutely delighted, having a wonderful time consuming the pastry.)*

ELAINE: Well. I'm glad. Enjoy.

> *(Lights start to fade as she looks back at the text. Takes another bite. She may well have a bit of chocolate or cream on her face by now.)*

ELAINE: Here: make my veil your sash; it is not mortal;

> You cannot, now, be drowned or suffer harm.

ELAINE AND MR. CARAGIANIS: *(Together.)* Only, the instant you lay hold of earth,

> Discard it, cast it far, far out from shore
>
> In the wine-dark sea again, and turn away."
>
> *(Lights fade to black.)*

END OF PLAY

Happy No-lidays

KEYTHE FARLEY

CHARACTERS

HE, twenty-five to thirty-five, a sweet slacker.
SHE, twenty-five to thirty-five, a sweet slacker.

SETTING

A couch and a Christmas tree.

TIME

The present.

. . .

At rise: She is watching television. He enters with a bowl of popcorn.

SHE: Oooh! Popping corn. Thank you.
　　(She kisses him. He sits next to her.)
HE: What are we watching?
SHE: *Charlie Brown Christmas.*
HE: Cool.
SHE: I love the dance sequence.
HE: Yep. Who's your favorite?
SHE: Violet.
HE: Yeah. Violet's a cool dancer.
SHE: Who's yours?
HE: Schroeder.
SHE: Shut up!
HE: What?
SHE: Schroeder doesn't dance.
HE: You don't know that.
SHE: True.
HE: I bet he's a great dancer.
SHE: Show me how Schroeder would dance.
HE: OK. Like this.
　　(He gets up and "raises the roof." She laughs at him.)
SHE: You are so weird.
HE: What?
SHE: Schroeder wouldn't raise the roof.
HE: Why not?
SHE: It's 1964. Nobody raised the roof for, like, thirty-five years.

HE: Schroeder's ahead of his time.

SHE: You are so weird.

HE: Come on. An eight-year-old kid who plays piano like that would totally be ahead of his time. Like Bowie.

SHE: Whatever.

(He sits. Pause. They watch TV for a moment.)

HE: So, what did you get me for Christmas?

SHE: I'm not telling.

HE: Why not?

SHE: It's a surprise.

HE: I'd tell you.

SHE: OK. What did you get me?

HE: I didn't get you anything, yet.

SHE: What?

HE: Which doesn't mean I won't.

SHE: OK.

(They watch and eat.)

HE: Your turn.

SHE: What?

HE: Your turn to tell.

SHE: No.

HE: I told you.

SHE: So?

HE: Quid pro quo.

SHE: No.

HE: No what?

SHE: No both.

HE: No quid pro quo?

SHE: Yes.

HE: And no, you didn't get me a present.

SHE: Not exactly, no.

(They watch and eat.)

HE: Doggone holidays.

SHE: Yeah.

HE: The whole marketing machine tells you that the only way to show you love someone is to spend money on them. The more you spend, the more you love.

SHE: And if you don't have money, you can't have love.

HE: And that's just plain wrong.

(They watch and eat.)

HE: What if we start our own holiday movement?

SHE: What?

HE: An antiholiday.

SHE: With no presents?

HE: No debt.

SHE: No shopping frenzy.

HE: All the love with none of the hassle.

SHE: Totally!

HE: We could run a commercial on TV during the shopping season. Check this out. Fade in on Santa's Village—only it's not the cute little town we're used to seeing—it's like a huge Ikea-sized factory. We fly in through the front loading bay, and we're at the nexus of the Santa operation. There's all these elves as far as the eye can see, and they're busting their humps to try to make the Christmas deadline.

SHE: And they're miserable.

HE: Yeah. Some are trying to figure how to put a PS3 together.

SHE: You gotta have a couple of them trying to tie a big bow on top of a Lexus.

HE: Right. That's funny.

SHE: Like they can't figure out how to tie a bow that's as big as they are.

HE: Right. Anyway, it's basically a sweatshop.

SHE: Right.

HE: It's horrible. Everyone's scrambling to make the deadline.

SHE: I get it. Where's Santa?

HE: He's smoking a pipe and slugging down one last hot chocolate for the road in his executive suite.

SHE: Right.

HE: He's the big boss. The beneficiary of the labor of the elfin hordes.

SHE: Wow.

HE: So we track him through the factory and he's slinging all these bogus Christmas phrases at the elves.

SHE: It's better to give than to receive.

HE: Right. And he's all, "Ho! Ho! Ho!" and stuff. And he gets into the sleigh and flies off into the night. Couple of cool shots of the sleigh going across the moon, and he lands the thing on someone's roof. He's all, "Ho! Ho! Ho!" and he pops down the chimney, and sees . . . us. We're waiting for him, and we're not happy.

SHE: We're not mad, though.

HE: No. But we're not happy, either. We're assured of ourselves.

SHE: I don't think being mad at Santa is going to get us anywhere.

HE: I got ya. Anyway, Santa sees us and goes, "Ho! Ho! Ho!" And we go, "No! No! No!"

SHE: Oh my God, I love it! "No. No. No." Not mad, though.

HE: No, no, no. Just firm and resolute "No. No. No." And we point him back up the chimney and send him on his way.

SHE: This is so cool. We tell materialism to go away.

HE: Right. And it could be a series of ads with all these different people all telling Santa, No. No. No.

SHE: You could show people in stores shopping like mad, and then a person could walk up to them and say "no, no, no" really gently.

HE: Or just a bunch of credit cards swiping until they finally come up declined. Then, "No. No. No."

SHE: Right. People stranded at airports.

SHE: Families fighting over Christmas dinner. All that stuff. And more.

SHE: No. No. No.

HE: No. No. No. And at the end of every ad the screen would fade to black, and a card that says Happy Holidays would pop up, but then the "H" in Holidays would get Xed-out and be replaced by an "N." So it says Happy No-lidays.

SHE: Happy No-lidays. I love it. Happy No-lidays, sweetie.

HE: Happy No-lidays, love.

(They kiss. They cuddle. Then:)

SHE: We need an icon.

HE: *(Chuckling.)* No. No. No.

SHE: Why not?

HE: No, no, no. I was just saying the slogan again. Yes! We need an icon.

SHE: A No-liday icon. Like Santa.

HE: Right. Anti-Claus!

SHE: How 'bout Madonna?

HE: What?

SHE: Madonna. She'd be perfect.

HE: How do you figure?

SHE: Well, her name, first of all.

HE: Madonna.

SHE: Yeah. Like the Virgin Mary? Madonna? You get the Christians right there.

HE: You think?

SHE: Plus, she's all into the kabala now, so you get the Jews, too.

HE: You're funny.

SHE: OK, so she may not have actual religious significance, but she's still a big name.

HE: True.

SHE: And she's got that song "Holiday."

HE: Would she change it to "No-liday"?

SHE: She'd have to. *(She sings.)* "No-li-dah-ee. Ce-le-bra-eet. It could be so nice. If I took a No-liday." Can't you see it?

HE: Yeah, I guess. Oh! You know what the problem with Madonna is?

SHE: Careful.

HE: As a No-liday icon, only.

SHE: OK.

HE: If Madonna was the spokesperson for the No-lidays, you couldn't have a tradition, because every year she'd want to change the holiday into something else.

SHE: Ooo. You're right. I know! What about Ellen DeGeneres?

HE: She's cool. k.d. lang?

SHE: She'd write some good No-liday songs, I bet. Ooo! I got it.

HE: Go ahead.

SHE: No. This one's perfect.

HE: Tell me.

SHE: No. You have to get all of the lesser candidates out of your system. Go.

HE: Umm . . . Charles Durning . . . Ed Asner . . . Mickey Rooney . . . Eminem . . . Jon Stewart . . .

SHE: William Shatner.

HE: Oh. My. God. William Shatner.

SHE: Consistent.

HE: Hungry for work.

SHE: Funny and serious at the same time.

HE: Great hair.

SHE: Same hair.

HE: William Shatner

SHE: William Shatner.

HE: You're a genius.

SHE: Thanks.

(They kiss. They eat popcorn and watch TV.)

SHE: What about the tree?

HE: Huh?

SHE: Can we keep the tree?

HE: Good question.

SHE: I love the tree.

HE: Yeah.

SHE: It's so pretty. And it smells so nice.

HE: Yeah. *(He regards the tree for a moment.)* How would you feel about a fern?

SHE: What?

HE: A No-liday fern. You could still decorate it. And it would live on from season to season.

SHE: But ferns are so hard to keep alive.

HE: That's part of it. You spend all your No-liday energy trying to keep the fern alive. The fern becomes the focus.

SHE: But what if it dies? No No-lidays? You're a No-liday failure?

HE: You're right.

SHE: I say we keep the tree. "Take Back the Tree."

HE: OK. But no decorations. Just the smell.

SHE: And some pretty lights.

HE: Lights, too, huh?

SHE: Yeah. They're too pretty to lose.

HE: They are pretty.

SHE: Turn off the TV.

(He turns off the TV.)

SHE: And the lamp.

(He turns off the lamp. The twinkle lights from the tree illuminate the scene. He sits next to her.)

HE: Wow.

SHE: You don't really want to give this up, do you?

HE: Not really.

SHE: I know what the holidays are for, even if the world has forgotten.

HE: *(A statement.)* You do.

SHE: I don't need to start a movement.

HE: Who needs the hassle?

SHE: Right. The real holidays are about new beginnings.

HE: True.

SHE: The real holidays are about hope. Hoping that the sun will come back.

HE: 'Cause it sure is cold now.

SHE: They're about love with a big L.

HE: And peace with a big P.

SHE: And family.

HE: Family.

(He produces a small black box from the popcorn bowl.)

HE: Will you be my family?

SHE: What? You said . . .

HE: I said I didn't get you a Christmas present. This is a family present. It's for this Christmas and forever.

SHE: It's beautiful. Wow.

HE: Will you be my family?

SHE: Yeah.

(They kiss.)

SHE: I'm glad you did this.

HE: Me too.

SHE: I'm gladder.

HE: Why?

SHE: I'm going to have a baby.

(Long pause. They just stare into each other's eyes.)

HE: I really didn't think you could top the ring.

SHE: What can I say?

HE: I love you.

SHE: I love you.

(They kiss and cuddle in the glow of twinkle lights.)

HE: Have you thought about names?

SHE: If it's a girl—Madonna. If it's a boy . . .

HE: William Shatner.

SHE: Yeah.

HE: Or Schroeder.

(Lights fade.)

END OF PLAY

I Have It

BEKAH BRUNSTETTER

Originally produced in Manhattan Theatre Source's
Estrogenius Festival, September 2007. Directed by Irene
Carroll. Cast: Lady—Caroline Parsons; George—Tom Rowen.

LADY, midtwenties. She wears a white dress that she took too long picking out.

GEORGE, midtwenties. He wears a nice shirt, buttoned all the way up.

SETTING

A park bench, of course. A nice day, of course. There are children, hot dogs. Homeless men who once spoke French. Acoustic guitars, grass stains, dead popsicle sticks. Presiding over all of it, a fat sun.

TIME

The present.

NOTES: Both characters come from good homes; both their dads have boats. George has always embraced his privileged upbringing; Lady has always rejected hers.

A slash (/) indicates that the next character begins to speak his or her line, overlapping the first speaker.

•   •   •

A park. Lady and George sit at nearly opposite ends of the bench. Do they know each other? We're not sure. A bright red balloon is tied to the arm near George. The balloon embarrasses him. Pause so we can hear the kids and smell the dogs and feel their uncomfortable silence before they speak.

LADY: I / thought your name was George.

GEORGE: It's a nice day. Very / supple.

LADY: What?

GEORGE: The day. It's nice.

LADY: I've seen worse.

GEORGE: Me too.

LADY: Wait, it's—supple?

GEORGE: No, yeah, I was trying to . . . think of . . . a different type of word to . . . apply to . . . this sort of weather, I guess, other than nice or, or pleasant, or good. And then I said supple.

LADY: Oh.

GEORGE: Don't you ever want to use different words than the ones you always do?

LADY: Uh . . . *yeah* . . . all the time—

GEORGE: Like all we ever use are the same words when there so *many*.

LADY: I mean, yeah, all I use are different words. I use diverse amounts of words all the time. I like to experiment. *(Pause.)* I was saying, uh, I thought your name was George.

GEORGE: It is.

LADY: But when, when we met, you said, you shook my hand / you said— "Hi, I'm Greg."

GEORGE: Greg is a VERSION of George. It's a casual way shorten the name. It's common. Lots of Georges do it. It's, it's normal.

LADY: Oh. S—sorry.

GEORGE: It's OK.

LADY: Did you notice that we hadn't said anything for two minutes?

GEORGE: N—nooo . . . *(Pause.)* We shouldn't talk because we feel like / we *have* to—

LADY: Wait, what? We shouldn't . . . no, we're supposed to be . . . aren't we supposed to be getting to know each other?

GEORGE: Yeah, I guess, I'm just saying let's not *force* it. *(Pause.)* Do you want some ice cream or something?

LADY: Why, am I boring?

GEORGE: Nooo.

LADY: Awesome. *(Pause. Lady doesn't know where to look, so she looks at the clouds.)* That cloud looks like my grandmother.

GEORGE: Which one?

LADY: Never mind. It moved. But it did.

(George scratches and rearranges his crotch. Lady doesn't see.)

LADY: So when was your last . . . I mean . . . when did it last . . . I mean / are you, right now . . . do you have it right now?

GEORGE: I don't really / want to . . . I don't want to get in to all . . . can we just

LADY: Yeah, no, I totally understand . . . Of course you don't / . . . that was . . . totally . . . inappropriate. I should be *shot*.

GEORGE: I mean, I'd kind of like to just sit here / with a pretty girl on a bench and watch the kids play.

LADY: Yeah, I should definitely just be shot. Somebody should just put a gun to my balls and *blow*.

(Pause. They look at each other.)

GEORGE: You have balls?

LADY: N—no, not . . . I just don't think it's *fair* that only people who actually have balls should be able to use the term. I think it limits our speech, I, I think we *all* have . . . metaphorical balls. Especially when you're trying to make a point, and I can't, I can't remember, what point I was trying to—wait. *(Pause.)* Did you just say I was pretty? *(Pause.)*

GEORGE: I can't remember.

LADY: You did. *(She smiles.)* You think I'm pretty.

GEORGE: Yeah, well, maybe.

(Lady gets excited.)

LADY: When you walked up, I thought, I hope that's him.

GEORGE: And I thought, I hope that's her.

LADY: *You* look like this boy I went to high school with who worked at Abercrombie and Fitch. He was a million feet tall and smelled like a forest. He was so hot. He like gave eight cheerleaders HPV or it coulda been from a toilet seat but I think it was him.

(She smiles, engaged in her talking. He clears his throat, looks off.)

LADY: . . . What?

GEORGE: Nothing. Could you not . . . talk about . . . Could you not . . . all the . . . just settle down.

LADY: *(Her face falls.)* . . . Settle down?

GEORGE: You're talking like . . . really loud. You're one of those girls / who—

LADY: Um, I'm not *any* kind of girl, OK? I am retardedly unique.

GEORGE: You brought me a *balloon.*

LADY: I thought it was unpredictable and cute. And, and given the NATURE of our RELATIONSHIP I just thought that—

GEORGE: Whoa. Relationship?

LADY: No, I mean, I mean the way that we *met,* the specifics of . . . I just thought that we already KNOW so much about each other, I mean, gross, intimate / details—

GEORGE: Shhh . . . do you have to talk so loud? There are like kids and parents.

(She is not talking loud at all, but she complies and starts to whisper.)

LADY: I'm just saying that we already know so much about our . . . so we might as well, we might as well, I don't know. Just be ourselves.

GEORGE: I'm being myself.

(Lady looks at his shirt.)

LADY: So am I. *(Pause.)* You always button the top button?

GEORGE: *Yeah.*

LADY: That looks uncomfortable.

(Pause. He unbuttons it.)

LADY: Well. I, um. I couldn't believe it, could you? When I found the . . . when I saw that there was an actual place where I could meet people who, who I already knew that . . . had the. Had it. So that I wouldn't have to . . . you know, have that awful conversation when . . . you're like, *I have to tell you something,* and they're like *what's with the superintense tone of voice like somebody's dog died, we just met?* And you're like *uh, before this goes any further,* and next thing you know you pass them on the street and they got their hand down the back of some girl's Old Navy Skinny Jeans. Have you had it?

GEORGE: Had what?

LADY: That awful conversation. The worst.

GEORGE: No.

LADY: *(Alarmed.)* Uh . . . wait . . . hello, you have to. It's a must.

GEORGE: No, I know. I haven't been, um, I've been . . . abstaining.

LADY: Oh. *(Pause.)* No, me too. *(Pause.)*

GEORGE: You are pretty, though. I can see why, um.

LADY: Why what?

GEORGE: Why you, um . . . why guys tend to . . . want to, uh—

LADY: Hey. Wait. Listen. Mine was a one—time—listen, I'm not some fucking . . . I, I make LOVE. I love with my WHOLE SELF. I don't go around, I'm not some fucking . . . I don't even wear THONGS. I read Christian romance novels! My dad voted for Bush!

GEORGE: Mine, too.

LADY: I was a virgin for a VERY LONG TIME. It took a whole lot for me to put out. There were like candles and some VERY choice words and a whole pecan pie.

GEORGE: Me too.

LADY: What, did you think I was—Some kind of—'cause I'm not. Do you want me to assume things about you, too? 'Cause I could. I could assume that you give really bad head and that you pee in the shower.

GEORGE: I wasn't trying to—

(Lady frantically digs through her purse and finds a bottle of bubbles. She blows them, relieving her angst. He watches. He is amused but doesn't know what to do with her.)

GEORGE: . . . Seriously?

LADY: I thought I was being spontaneous. I thought you might think it's cute. *(She blows more bubbles. She watches him.)* Yay. I'm embarrassing you.

GEORGE: I just don't . . . I don't like *yelling*. Especially in public. It's embarrassing and like the worst thing ever.

LADY: No it's not. There are lots of things worse.

GEORGE: I know.

LADY: Cervical cancer. *(Pause.)* And If we didn't yell in public, when even would we yell? It's *convenient.*

GEORGE: Uh—*private*. People are supposed to yell at each other in PRIVATE like everybody else.

LADY: Boring.

GEORGE: Normal.

LADY: Tomato.

GEORGE: What?

LADY: Never mind. You don't get it.

GEORGE: Do you think you speak in some complex way that I can't understand?

LADY: I think you read whatever everybody else is reading. I think you *loved* the *DaVinci Code*. I think you don't like fake meat.

GEORGE: Really. I think you watch reality TV.

LADY: I—I do NOT. I fucking NEVER watch reality TV!

GEORGE: OK, yeah, well, maybe you're a little too . . . you might be . . . for my taste . . . I'm just saying—

LADY: Listen, you don't *know* me. You have no idea whether or not I'm your type! How can you already *know?* There is no way after five minutes that you could already presume to know that I am an unideal person to spend sixty-seven percent of your time with. You don't know the power of my blueberry pancakes EVEN when they're a little burnt, in fact, they are BETTER that way. You don't know the depths that I . . . how DEEP I, I am VERY DEEP.

GEORGE: Please . . . please stop yelling. People are *staring.*

LADY: *(Standing, yelling.)* WHAT?

GEORGE: I was just trying to—

LADY: WHAT?

GEORGE: *(Yells.)* I was just trying to tell you that you're pretty! *(Pause. He acknowledges quietly the fact that he just yelled. It seems to have felt kind of good.)* Before you flipped out and got mad. You're not supposed to get mad at people you don't know. It's not polite.
(Pause.)

LADY: I am *very* polite.

GEORGE: Then LISTEN. I was just trying to say before that, that when I was little—I hate it when people say that: *when I was little*—but when I was little, my mom had an old piano with a bunch of old books full of sheet music. When I was first starting lessons, when I couldn't do the hard stuff. OK?

LADY: OK.

GEORGE: And on one of the covers there was this woman from like the 1920s sitting at a piano in a purple dress. You could only see the side of her face, her profile—but I thought she was the most beautiful, the most, um, she had a long neck and delicate, um, delicate eyelashes like strong enough to hold just one snowflake, and, and, I was just going to say that you remind me of her. That's all. When you look . . . when you look that way. Do it. Like this. *(Gently, he takes her chin between his fingers and moves her face profile. He smiles and inspects.)* Right there.

(Pause. Lady smiles, uncomfortable.)

LADY: I hate it when people say, "Oh my God, I had the craziest dream last night," and then you have to sit there listening to them talk to you about their dream, which is like, impossible, you CAN'T describe a dream 'cause it's a feeling you can't grab with words. But they keep going and going until they get to the part where they can't remember or they woke up. And you say, yeah, wow. *(Pause.)* You play the piano?

(He nods. She likes this.)

LADY: I dreamt last night I got shot in the head.

GEORGE: . . . Oh. Wow.

LADY: Don't pretend.

GEORGE: No. Seriously. Wow.

(Pause.)

LADY: I just think we should share our stories. That's all I was trying to get us to do.

GEORGE: What's to tell?

LADY: Specifics.

GEORGE: I don't know.

LADY: This was outside the Louvre.

GEORGE: What was?

LADY: Mine.

GEORGE: Paris. What were you doing there?

LADY: Irreversible mistakes. *(Pause.)* That place has, or it had, a tendency to make you . . . Pants come off. Or dresses up. He was . . . he said . . . Oh my God. *(Pause.)* I can't even remember. I've forgotten. *(Pause.)* But I'm sure it was him, because before that, there wasn't any . . . there weren't any, um . . . there hadn't been, for a while . . . yeah, it was definitely . . . *(Pause.)* OK, you go now.

GEORGE: I don't know.

LADY: Oh, come on.

GEORGE: No. I really don't know.

LADY: Seriously?

GEORGE: I don't really / want to—

LADY: Then why are you even *here?* You do. You DO want to talk about it or you wouldn't have, you wouldn't have reached out like you did. We wouldn't be on this bench.

(Pause.)

GEORGE: There was a time when I was . . . I'm not . . . I'm not proud of . . . yeah. There were a lot of . . . quite a few—

LADY: Temptations.

GEORGE: Yeah and I felt invincible.

LADY: As opposed to?

GEORGE: Small?

(Pause. Lady thinks. She thinks too much.)

LADY: I know what you mean.

GEORGE: I know.

LADY: Yeah. *(Pause.)* I've—wasted a lot of time. I—I've spent a good part of my life sitting around waiting for someone to fall in love with me. Like . . . now? How about now? Has it happened yet? But I'm always, like . . . looking out of the corner of my eye to see if it's happening. Is anyone looking? No one is. Not yet, not right now, they're looking at that other girl whose prettiness warrants her strangeness in a very exact way that makes her glow. By the way, We have no control over that glow. It's not something you can just *acquire* if it's not something you already have.

GEORGE: That's what's so great about it.

LADY: Yeah, well. But when I get tired of waiting for . . . I try and . . . I try and *force*—

GEORGE: That's not how it works. You can't force it. You just have to like, BE.

LADY: I'm, I'm TRYING. I seem to be completely incapable of just BEING. And now look what . . . *(Pause.)* I just, I just don't think it's fair, you know? None of this is fair. When you think about all the people who are fine, who every night are out, like with a different person—

GEORGE: Yeah. Your dad, I mean, my dad—dads make you feel like they'll protect you from anything. Like you're never going to die.

LADY: Yeah, and the one time—the *one time* I, I mean, I'm a good girl, I, I know right from wrong, I know sloppy from careful, why can't all the other people who . . . and you think, *this* is what happens when you love for a minute? When you finally let yourself do it? Whatever it is that makes you feel . . . in your stomach . . . compels you to . . . take the love outside of yourself and like put it *into* or *onto* the other person? With your body? Let yourself go? What is that, why does it feel like that? And the one time I, I just don't think . . . *(Pause. She starts to cry.)* I just don't think it should mean that I have to be alone. Why does it feel like that?

GEORGE: I, I don't know.

LADY: It's not fair.

(George reaches across the bench and takes her hand. They sit.)

GEORGE: I think I dreamt last night that you and I were on my dad's boat?

LADY: But we hadn't met yet.

GEORGE: But I had seen your picture. Yeah, it was definitely you. We were wearing, yeah, we were wearing lifesavers, big yellow ones, and, and were about to jump into the water, and we did. There were friendly snakes and flowers, all over. The water felt nice. Like it how it feels when you're little. When you don't know anything yet. Before anything has happened.

(Pause. They keep holding hands. Lady dries her tears.)

LADY: So what would happen if, if you and I . . . if you and I . . .

GEORGE: If we—

LADY: Do we just—

GEORGE: I think we would just . . . pass it . . . back and forth.

LADY: Yeah. I give it to you.

GEORGE: Yeah and then you give it to me.

LADY: Yeah and then we just keep passing it back and forth. Between each other.

GEORGE: Yeah. We would just keep passing it back and forth.

(Lights.)

END OF PLAY

Paris' Snatch

BRIAN DYKSTRA

Originally produced at 440 Studios Black Box, New York City,
May 3–5, 2007, as part of POP! Riffs, rants,
and ramblings on the current state of popular
cultural affairs. Directed by Jared Fine. Cast: Austin—
J. Eric Fisher; Alison—Kimberly Rossiter.

Based on recent events.

CHARACTERS

AUSTIN, early twenties. Gadget savvy. A product of the popular culture.
ALISON, early twenties. Nagged by the existential questions. A victim of
the popular culture.

SETTING

A street. Maybe a bench, or an apartment stoop. Outside. In the city. The
setting is nondescript. The weather is "fine." The skies are not bright sunlight nor dark overcast.

TIME

The present.

•   •   •

*Alison in onstage. She is texting someone, listening to her iPod. Austin rushes
on with his cell-phone camera, showing the screen to Alison.*

AUSTIN: Look! Look! Look!
   (He shoves the screen into her face.)
ALISON: What?
AUSTIN: Will you . . . Just look at it. Will you look at it!
ALISON: Be a little forceful.
AUSTIN: Just . . . come on.
   (She turns off her iPod, studies the picture for a moment.)
ALISON: What am I . . . *(Then realizes what she's looking at.)* Jesus.
AUSTIN: I know.
   (She removes her ear buds.)
ALISON: Jesus.
AUSTIN: Totally.
ALISON: Why are you—
AUSTIN: Total double play! A two-cooch sandwich. Wham-bam-thank-you-
   ma'am—double-clam!
ALISON: Why are you showing this to me?
AUSTIN: What? Really?
ALISON: Why are you showing me this?

AUSTIN: Are you kidding?

ALISON: No, I'm asking.

AUSTIN: Do you know what this is?

ALISON: Yes.

AUSTIN: Then I don't understand your question.

ALISON: Austin, why do you think I want to see a double upskirt, sans panties, crawling out of a car?

AUSTIN: Are you kidding me?

ALISON: I'm not a lesbian.

AUSTIN: No, I—

ALISON: I was a little bi-curious for like ten minutes, so what. OK, I never should have posted that thing, but even if I was, why do you think I want to look at something like that? Porn is kind of more up your alley. Or so I've heard.

AUSTIN: Do you know who these vaginas belong to?

(Alison studies the image once again.)

ALISON: How the fuck would I know that?

AUSTIN: That is, that picture, that is the golden . . . thing, right there, is what that is—Chalice! That's the Holy Grail. The end of the rainbow, my friend. Pot of gold. Not an evil leprechaun guarding it in sight.

ALISON: Really? Looks to me like a couple of shy beavers peeking out from behind a curtain. And the bucktooth one needs a little trim.

AUSTIN: Ha-ha-ha, she said "trim."

ALISON: Austin? Are you that starved for a little action?

AUSTIN: That's Britney Spears. Let me just say that.

ALISON: Really?

AUSTIN: And the little box next to her is Paris Hilton.

ALISON: No way!

AUSTIN: Way.

ALISON: How did you get this?

AUSTIN: Walking by that thing, that fashion week thing, the one sponsored by Google.

ALISON: And they were just getting out of a limo? Together?

AUSTIN: There was this group of paparazzi and I couldn't get by, so I kind of walked into the street, where a fuckin' douche bag yakking on his Blue-tooth in a Prius—oh, you're so advanced—almost ran me over. But I took out my Treo, you know, in case there was a shot to be shot. Or, actually,

I thought I'd just shoot the paparazzi and post it on MySpace, you know, kind of a "look how gross these people can be" kind of thing.

ALISON: Right.

AUSTIN: And I'm lining up the shot when the door opens on the street side. The street side, can you believe it? And there's Paris and Britney scooting out to run past me into the building across the street, but like, Paris drops her Blackberry, or Sidekick, no Blackberry, and hollers for Britney to hold up and the paparazzi start to run around the car, so they dart out, towards me and that's when I shoot the shot. Click. Pussy, pussy.

ALISON: Oh, right. They're doing that BFF campaign for that "new friends call free" thing.

AUSTIN: I think it was for that other one.

ALISON: What the "AOL LOL" campaign or the "OMG No to SUVs" PSA?

AUSTIN: I think—

ALISON: Or aren't they joining the Mac versus PC campaign? I think somebody texted me about that, where they're both going to end up with the cute Mac guy. Or was with that Carmen Electra?

AUSTIN: Isn't there a iPod Wi-Fi online dating service through iTunes?

ALISON: That's still in the works.

AUSTIN: Oh.

ALISON: And why would Paris and Britney advertise a dating service?

AUSTIN: Money.

ALISON: Oh, right.

AUSTIN: So, what do you think?

ALISON: About your shot?

AUSTIN: Yeah.

ALISON: I think you captured bookend beavers trying to escape captivity.

AUSTIN: Totally.

ALISON: Why, what do you think?

AUSTIN: I think I'm going to write about this shit on my blog and get so much traffic the tabloids will be pounding down my door to hand me checks with a bunch of zeros. That's what I think.

ALISON: Not going to happen.

AUSTIN: Jealous?

ALISON: Practical.

AUSTIN: This is the kind of shit tabloids eat up.

ALISON: Austin?

AUSTIN: What?

ALISON: How do we know who those punnanis belong to?

AUSTIN: What? I just told you.

ALISON: Yeah, but how do we know?

AUSTIN: Who else could they be?

ALISON: Seriously?

AUSTIN: Yeah.

ALISON: Half the population.

AUSTIN: What?

ALISON: You didn't get their faces.

AUSTIN: What?

ALISON: You're too close up. Yes, I see: A snatch, and another snatch. But if there isn't a face to put to those coots, who's going to believe it's really them?

AUSTIN: Really?

ALISON: Duh.

AUSTIN: Can't we compare?

ALISON: Compare what?

AUSTIN: Come on. Both those vaginas are on file. We got sex tapes and/or up-skirts from both those little stanks.

ALISON: So what are you suggesting? Somebody run pictures that we can prove are the real deal and side by side compare them to the ones you shot?

AUSTIN: Why not?

ALISON: Well, if vaginas are indeed like fingerprints . . . you didn't get enough detail.

AUSTIN: What are you talking about?

ALISON: You know what? Good luck with it.

AUSTIN: Ali.

ALISON: What?

AUSTIN: You're such a fucking downer.

ALISON: Not since we adjusted my meds.

AUSTIN: You think this is worthless?

ALISON: Yeah.

AUSTIN: Fuck.

ALISON: Yeah. It's too bad.

AUSTIN: I'm going back.

ALISON: Good luck.

AUSTIN: What are you doing?

ALISON: Waiting.

AUSTIN: For what?

ALISON: My life to have meaning.

AUSTIN: Huh. Good luck with that.

ALISON: Yeah . . . you too.

(*Austin leaves. Alison waits. She checks her phone, answers a text message— or not. Reinserts her ear buds, plays her iPod. Waits. Fade to blackout.*)

END OF PLAY

The Passion of
Merlin and Vivien
in the Forest of
Broceliande

DON NIGRO

CHARACTERS

MERLIN, a sorcerer.

VIVIEN, his apprentice.

SETTING

The enchanted Forest of Broceliande. One mossy tree stump will do.

TIME

Once upon.

> A storm was coming, but the winds were still,
> and in the wild woods of Broceliande,
> before an oak, so hollow, huge, and old
> it looked a tower of ivied masonwork,
> at Merlin's feet the wily Vivien lay.
>
> —*Tennyson, "Merlin and Vivien"*

. . .

Sound of birds and approaching thunder. Lights up on the ancient and enchanted Forest of Broceliande. Leaf shadows. There is an old, moss-covered tree stump. Merlin and Vivien have been walking in the forest. She is quite young. He is probably not the incredibly ancient, white-bearded figure one has become familiar with elsewhere, but he's quite a bit older than she is.

MERLIN: It's begun to rain. Why did you insist on wandering so deep into the forest? I'm too old to walk this far.

VIVIEN: We can rest here. This is a good place.

MERLIN: *(Sitting down on the stump.)* My mouth is dry as old chicken bones.

VIVIEN: *(Placing one hand at her bodice.)* Perhaps you'd like to suckle at my breasts.

MERLIN: What I would like does not signify much, I think.

VIVIEN: *(Producing a small flask from between her breasts.)* I've brought some wine. *(She holds the flask out to him.)* Here.

MERLIN: *(Taking the flask.)* What a clever girl you are. Where did you get that?

VIVIEN: It's my very own creation.

MERLIN: *(Removes the cork, sniffs the rim, then drinks.)* This is quite unusual. It has a woody taste. It's potent stuff. It feels alive, going down.

VIVIEN: It is alive.

MERLIN: I detect bat wing. A touch of wormwood. Flowering cherry. And something else. Acorns, perhaps?

VIVIEN: Teach me something.

MERLIN: I've taught you everything I know. And several things I don't know. I've taught you a number of things I made up on the spot, just to keep you amused.

VIVIEN: No. Not everything. Not yet.

MERLIN: What knowledge you don't have, you know how to get now. One doesn't transfer knowledge to another so much as nurture the ability to find it for themselves. I've never had a better student.

VIVIEN: Not even Arthur?

MERLIN: Magic was not his specialty. But you've always seemed to know what I'm going to show you before I open my mouth. As if I'm just confirming something you're remembering from a past life. And you're absolutely ravenous. You're a girl who devours knowledge like a beautiful, starved little animal.

VIVIEN: Your eyes devour me. You have beautiful, sad eyes.

MERLIN: They never tire of watching you. Your moods are like casting runes. I can never predict what the next configuration will be. Your mind is flowing water. You're deeper than the lake I found you swimming naked in.

VIVIEN: You desired me then.

MERLIN: Did I?

VIVIEN: You desire me now.

MERLIN: Do you think me such a fool?

VIVIEN: You think a man's a fool if he desires me?

MERLIN: All desire is foolish, but an old man's love is a ridiculous, pathetic thing.

VIVIEN: You're not that old.

MERLIN: Compared to you I'm older than Stonehenge.

VIVIEN: I thought you built Stonehenge.

MERLIN: A rumor circulated by the ignorant. *(He takes another drink, looks at her.)* Why have you lured me to this place?

VIVIEN: Don't you know? I thought you could see the past, the present, and the future all laid out before you like a pack of cards.

MERLIN: Cards haven't been invented yet. And it's a dangerous and melancholy thing to look too deeply into the darkened mirror of one's own fate.

VIVIEN: I hope you understand how much you've meant to me.

MERLIN: That is a rather ominous beginning.

VIVIEN: You've been so good to me. So kind and patient. You've made me laugh a thousand times.

MERLIN: There's been much laughter in our friendship. Your company is all that's saved me from despair.

VIVIEN: When I've fallen asleep in your arms, you've stroked my hair so tenderly. I've been completely at your mercy, and not once have you taken advantage.

MERLIN: You've trusted me. Despite the fact I've taught you to trust nobody. It's a paradox. And so are you. You are the Lady of Enigmas. You live in a room filled with mirrors. Sometimes when I look in your eyes it seems that you're the old one, and I'm the child. And yet, for a child, my joints are very stiff.

VIVIEN: We mostly speak in jokes and parables, riddles and spells. We've seldom spoken of our feelings, you and I. And yet—

MERLIN: And yet what? An old man. A young girl. There's only one conclusion possible.

VIVIEN: (Holding in her fingers a locket that's suspended on a chain around her neck.) You gave me this locket I wear always, on a chain round my neck.

MERLIN: A charm, to keep you safe. It's what I do.

VIVIEN: I want to give you something.

MERLIN: Before you go away, you mean? I'd rather you kept the gift and stayed a while.

VIVIEN: Everything goes away. You taught me that.

MERLIN: (Holding out his hands, grasping and relaxing his fingers.) What's the matter with my hands? They feel like claws.

VIVIEN: I hope you'll understand this gift. Accept it in the spirit in which it's given.

MERLIN: My feet are heavy. The bones of my heels feel rooted to the ground.

VIVIEN: The potion's working now.

MERLIN: (Looking at her.) The wine. You put something in the wine.

VIVIEN: It's all right. Don't be alarmed.

MERLIN: What have you done? What's happening to me?

VIVIEN: It's nothing to worry about. You're turning into a tree.

MERLIN: A tree? I'm turning into a tree?

VIVIEN: The transformation should be relatively painless. You'll stiffen up. Grow roots from the bones in your feet, into the ground. Your skin will turn to bark. Leaves will sprout from your fingers. Ravens will nest in your hair.

MERLIN: You tell me I've been kind to you, and taught you everything I know, and this is what you give me in return? You turn me into a tree?

VIVIEN: Just what return were you expecting from me? Didn't you teach me that love's only recompense is the privilege of having loved?

MERLIN: Don't speak to me of love. I'm growing bark.

VIVIEN: I do love you. I do.

MERLIN: You're mocking me.

VIVIEN: You are the one true passion of my life.

MERLIN: The one true passion? I'm your one true passion?

VIVIEN: I swear it's true.

MERLIN: You wanted my magic. That's all. You wanted the power to do things. I've taught you how to get what you want. And now you use it against me. I don't know why I should be astonished at this treachery, but I am.

VIVIEN: I wanted to know. And you wanted to teach me. Nobody forced you.

MERLIN: I wanted to be close to you. I wanted to smell your hair. I wanted to feel the warmth of your body when you stood near me, leaned on me, fell asleep in my arms like a child. I suppose it's my just punishment. When an old man loves, what can he expect but humiliation?

VIVIEN: I never wished you any harm.

MERLIN: And now you have my magic, you don't need me anymore.

VIVIEN: It isn't like that.

MERLIN: The student kills the teacher. I must have known. I must have always known. I saw it, and willed my own ignorance, so as to keep you near me for a while.

VIVIEN: It won't be so bad here, in the forest. You taught me to love the trees. You taught me trees are holy things, with souls.

MERLIN: (As his arms begin twisting upwards, palms up, fingers spread like twigs.) I said they have souls. I didn't say I wanted to be one.

VIVIEN: Listen to me, if you love me, and try to understand. I can't compete with you. I need to use the power I have inside me, and I can't when you're around. We'll always be compared, one to another. I'll always be in your shadow. I must have room to live. To be myself. To fashion my own adventures. And it's not as if we'll ever really be apart. You'll always be with me, whispering in my head. I'll never get rid of you.

MERLIN: I won't be in your head. I'll be here in the woods, being shat on by sparrows and pissed on by wolves. What's wrong with my arms? What's happening to my arms?

VIVIEN: Your arms will turn to lovely gnarled branches. You'll make the finest tree in all the enchanted Forest of Broceliande. You'll be the Tree of

Knowledge. Squirrels will run up and down you, chattering. Deer will take shelter by you in the rain. You've always liked trees and animals better than people. You'll be among your friends. Oh, please don't hate me.

MERLIN: I'm having trouble speaking.

VIVIEN: I need to go now. I hope you won't forget me.

MERLIN: What else will I have to think about?

VIVIEN: In all this time, you know, you never kissed me. Never once.

MERLIN: I never dared. I feared what it would make me feel.

VIVIEN: Well, there's no harm in it now.

(*She kisses him very tenderly on the lips. Then she takes the chain from around her neck and hangs the locket carefully on his upturned, clawlike hand.*)

VIVIEN: A charm to keep you safe. It's what I do. I must go and have adventures now.

(*She goes. Sound of birds, and the rain.*)

MERLIN: Yes. Well. Whose fault is this? Not hers. She's simply being who she must. What other expectation can a person have, who loves? (*Pause.*) The rain falls in the Forest of Broceliande. I can feel the moisture, drawing up from the ground through my roots. Strange nourishment. I must not think of her. Her face. The smell of her hair. Her eyes. The warmth of her next to me. Her breath on my lips. Her kiss. These illusions, in the enchanted forest. All right, squirrels. Do your worst. Bring your children. Come and build nests in me. (*Pause.*) How proud of her I am.

(*The light fades on him and goes out. Sound of birds and rain in the darkness.*)

END OF PLAY

Signs of Life

FREDERICK STROPPEL

Originally produced at the Theatre Artists Workshop,
Norwalk, Connecticut, May 2007, as part of Four Plays
and a Film, an evening of one-acts by Frederick Stroppel.
Directed by Joanna Keylock. Cast: Miles—Norman Marshall;
Virginia—Nadine Willig.

VIRGINIA, a middle-aged widow, who has a new love in her life, but still harbors issues.

MILES, Virginia's fiancé, a pharmacist, who doesn't quite know what he's getting into.

SETTING

A cemetery.

TIME

The present.

• • •

Virginia enters, carrying flowers. Her fiancé, Miles, follows her on.

MILES: This is a beautiful cemetery.

VIRGINIA: Yes, I like the fact that you can see the skyline from here. Sheldon always loved the city. He never worked there, but he had big dreams. He used to say, "Someday I'm going to own that city." Poor silly little man.

MILES: *(Points off.)* Big funeral going on over there.

VIRGINIA: Probably Italian. They make such a fuss. You'd think nobody ever died before. *(Looks around.)* My, this place is really filling up. When I bought Sheldon's plot, there were just a couple of graves, and now . . .

MILES: Business is booming.

VIRGINIA: Bunch of Johnny-come-latelies. *(Points to various gravestones.)* Look at these, with the pictures on them. So creepy. *(Points to tombstone.)* And this is Sheldon.

MILES: Oh . . . Yes. *(Reads the stone.)* Born in 1943 . . . So he was young.

VIRGINIA: Flu.

MILES: Really? Flu?

VIRGINIA: He was a weak man. In many ways.

MILES: Nice stone.

VIRGINIA: We had twenty-one wonderful years together. *(To grave.)* So—you're surprised to see me, huh?

MILES: What?

VIRGINIA: I'm talking to . . .

(Points to grave.)

MILES: Oh.

VIRGINIA: He usually sees me Easter, Christmas, the anniversary of his death . . . So he's probably confused that I'm suddenly here today.

MILES: Right. Although, it's not like he has a calendar down there.

VIRGINIA: *(Quite serious.)* He doesn't need a calendar. He's one with the earth.

MILES: Of course.

VIRGINIA: *(Back to grave.)* Sheldon? Sheldon! We brought you some flowers. You'd be amazed how inexpensive these are in the supermarket. All those years the florists were ripping us off . . .

(Miles tactfully backs away to give her privacy.)

VIRGINIA: Let's see, what's new? Jody's still in college, she's a sophomore now. She had a little pregnancy scare, but that's all over. Jason is doing something with computers, websites or blogs or something; I don't understand it, but he's making money . . . We painted the dining room; cream walls, with a sea-foam trim. I don't really like it, but . . . Anyway, I brought someone to meet you. This is Miles. I told you about him. *(To Miles.)* Miles. Come here. He wants to see you.

MILES: He wants to . . . ?

VIRGINIA: Yes, come over.

(Miles walks over hesitantly.)

VIRGINIA: No, on this side. He's blind in that eye.

MILES: *(Humoring her.)* Okaay . . .

(Miles moves over to the other side.)

VIRGINIA: *(To grave.)* So, there he is. Isn't he handsome? He's a doctor.

MILES: I'm a pharmacist . . .

VIRGINIA: *(Insists.)* A *doctor*. He has a practice in the city.

MILES: Queens . . .

VIRGINIA: *(To Miles.)* Honey? Just agree with me?

(Miles nods. Virginia turns back to the grave.)

VIRGINIA: So we've been seeing each other a while, and having some fun—he's good company, very easygoing, has a great sense of humor . . . Miles, tell him that joke.

MILES: Joke?

VIRGINIA: The one about the priest at the convent.

MILES: *(Reluctant.)* I don't think it'll work in this setting . . .

VIRGINIA: Oh, come on, it's funny.

MILES: Well . . . *(Clears his throat.)* See, this priest is visiting a convent, and the nun is giving him a tour, and they're walking down a hallway with all these paintings of saints and stuff, and the nun is describing them as they go along, and she's saying "This is the Virgin of Pompeii," and "This is the Virgin of Lourdes," and "This is the Virgin of, whatever, Fatima," and then the priest stops at one painting, and he says, "What Virgin is this?" and the nun says, "Oh, that's no virgin, that's the Mother Superior."

(Beat. Virginia laughs helpfully.)

VIRGINIA: (To grave.) So she was no virgin, apparently.

MILES: Well, maybe she was, but the way the nun phrased it . . .

VIRGINIA: You don't have to explain it to *me*, I get it. (To grave, seriously.) Anyway, the reason we're here is, we've been going out for a while, and we enjoy each other's company, and we're not getting any younger, so we've decided to get married. And we'd like to ask for your permission. And your blessing.

(Long beat.)

MILES: (Chiming in.) I'll take good care of her. I promise.

(Another long beat.)

MILES: (After a polite interval.) OK, so, should we move on . . . ?

VIRGINIA: Not yet—I'm waiting.

MILES: Waiting for what?

VIRGINIA: For a sign.

MILES: A sign of what?

VIRGINIA: A sign of his blessing.

MILES: What kind of sign?

VIRGINIA: Like a dove. Or a flash of lightning, or something.

MILES: (Smiles.) You really think . . . ?

(As Virginia glares at him, he grows serious.)

MILES: Yes, well, I suppose we could wait a few minutes. Probably takes a little time to give a sign. Especially if you've been dead a while.

(They wait.)

MILES: The sky is really blue today. That could be a sign.

VIRGINIA: (Not buying.) It was blue before.

(Beat.)

MILES: Look, a chipmunk! You don't see those every day.

(Virginia keeps looking. Nothing happens. She is growing increasingly irritated.)

MILES: Sometimes signs are hard to read. Like the handwriting on a prescription. Ha.

(She doesn't laugh.)

MILES: No, but seriously, he may be giving a very clear sign, but we're not seeing it. Messages can get garbled between worlds. It might be just the slightest breeze in your hair, or a dandelion spider floating by.

VIRGINIA: *(Scornful.)* A dandelion spider?

MILES: Anyway, he loved you, right?—and he would want you to be happy, so I'm sure he blesses our union.

VIRGINIA: Oh, are you? Are you so very sure? You didn't even know him! *(Seething.)* I know him. And this is just typical. The petty, spiteful little bastard. *(To the grave.)* That's right, I'm talking about you! What, you don't approve? He's not good enough? And I suppose you were? I suppose in all the years I knew you, you were something other than a cheap, pompous, mealy-mouthed, underachieving loser!

MILES: Virginia, please, I don't think this is the time or the place . . .

VIRGINIA: This is exactly the time and the place! This is where he's buried, and this is where we're going to settle some scores! He was never supportive of me from day one, and he hasn't changed. Always judging me, always thought he did me a big favor by marrying me . . . *(To grave.)* You said I'd never find anybody to take your place, remember? Well, I have. Feast your eyes. He's a real man, and he's alive, which is more than I can say for you!

MILES: *(Embarrassed.)* I think we might want to calm down . . .

VIRGINIA: I'll calm down, as soon as I get a couple of things off my chest. This son-of-a-bitch never appreciated what a gift he had in me. Never took a word of my advice. I told him to get a flu shot, but he wouldn't listen. Thought he was so smart. *(To grave.)* Loser!

MILES: You have no idea how well your voice carries.

VIRGINIA: Well, I want to make sure he hears me. He's six feet under, you know.

MILES: Those people over there are trying to bury a family member . . .

VIRGINIA: They're all in the mob, who cares about them? *(To grave.)* That's right, I finally have a real relationship, a caring, giving bond between equals, where we support each other, and listen to each other . . .

MILES: Honey . . .

VIRGINIA: Not now! *(To grave.)* And I'll tell you something else: He knows how to satisfy a woman. You know what he does that you could never manage? *(To Miles.)* Tell him. Tell him how you pleasure me.

MILES: *(Backing away.)* I don't . . .

VIRGINIA: No, he needs to know. It would be an education for him. *(To the grave.)* It's called foreplay, Sheldon! Scented oils, erotic poetry, and every position under the sun. We're halfway through the Kama Sutra, and it's full speed ahead!

MILES: Virginia, please, could you keep it down?

VIRGINIA: *(Laughing, to the grave.)* *I* can keep it down, but *he* can't—you know what I'm saying? Pure testosterone, 24/7. And he's not afraid of his feminine side, either. We've done all kinds of gender role-play, and it's been liberating for both of us. He knows what it's like to be penetrated . . .

MILES: *(Pulling her aside.)* Jesus Christ! Enough! We're in a cemetery, for God's sake!

VIRGINIA: I'm sorry if I'm making a scene, but he knows just how to push my buttons.

MILES: He hasn't said a word. For all you know, he might not even be down there.

VIRGINIA: *(Scornful.)* Where do you think he is? Heaven? Grow up! Of course he's down there, watching us, with a big Cheshire-cat grin plastered on his skull, enjoying himself. He thinks he's safe, we can't touch him, the arrogant prick. Somebody really ought to piss on his grave. *(An idea.)* Go ahead, Miles, you do it.

MILES: What? No . . .

VIRGINIA: Come on, take a nice long whiz all over his name. Let him know what it feels like.

(Virginia tries to unzip his fly.)

MILES: No, stop!

VIRGINIA: All right, *I'll* do it. I'm not shy.

(Virginia starts to hike up her skirt and squat over the grave. Miles pulls her away.)

MILES: Virginia—what are you doing?

VIRGINIA: I'm trying to make a point. You don't have to watch if you're squeamish.

MILES: This is very unseemly.

VIRGINIA: Oh, "unseemly." Listen to the big fancy pharmacist talk! What— am I embarrassing you? Are you passing judgment on me, too?

MILES: No, no, I'm just saying, it's time to move on. The past is past.

VIRGINIA: No, it isn't! The past is never past. If the past were past, we wouldn't need cemeteries. We could just dump everybody in a landfill and be done with them. But we're never done with them. They hang on like barnacles, they won't let go.

MILES: *(Reasonably.)* I think you're the one who won't let go. You're clinging to these old bitter memories, letting them gnaw at your insides, when the healthy thing to do is put them aside and look to the future. That's the only way you can be free.

(Virginia stares at him in wonder.)

VIRGINIA: That's about the most asinine thing I ever heard. Twenty-one years I was married to that asshole. You expect me to just forget? How stupid can you be?

MILES: I'm not stupid.

VIRGINIA: Well, you're not a *doctor*, are you?

MILES: Look, I don't want to fight with you.

VIRGINIA: We're not fighting. I'm calling you an idiot—there's nothing to argue about there.

(Beat.)

MILES: Maybe we're rushing into this marriage a little too quickly.

VIRGINIA: Maybe we are. I already spent a quarter of a century with one bone-head, I certainly don't need to get stuck with another one.

MILES: Fine—I'm leaving. Why don't you just stay here with your beloved Sheldon and talk over old times?

VIRGINIA: And why don't you just go to take a flying—

(She stops as she looks out at the sky.)

VIRGINIA: Look, what's that?

MILES: *(Amazed.)* It's a rainbow!

VIRGINIA: A rainbow in a blue sky—that's a sign! *(To the grave.)* Well—that's better. You certainly took your time about it. *(She takes Miles's hand.)* Isn't it beautiful! *(Sighs.)* We're going to be so happy together!

(She hugs Miles. He looks very uneasy.)

END OF PLAY

Skin & Bones

JULIAN SHEPPARD

Originally commissioned and produced by the stageFARM, at Cherry Lane Theatre, New York City, October 4– December 1, 2007, as part of Vengeance, a series of short plays. Directed by Ari Edelson. Cast: Jesse—Lisa Joyce; Alex—Michael Mosley.

CHARACTERS

    ALEX, man, thirties to forties.

    JESSE, woman, twenties.

SETTING

    Some place.

TIME

    Some time.

> My life is full of choices still
> Like when to kiss and when to kill
>
> —*Leslie Rankine*

. . .

A man in a small room. Two doors, one at either end. There is one chair. A large duffel bag is in the corner. A woman walls through one door wearing a mask, carrying another large, very heavy duffel bag.

ALEX: You got the skin?

    (The woman nods, pulls off the mask, and drops the bag at Alex's feet. It makes an odd sound when she does.)

ALEX: You didn't get it clean?

JESSE: I was rushed.

ALEX: We're on a schedule here.

JESSE: You'll sort it out, you're good at sorting things out.

ALEX: Any probs?

JESSE: Nothing major.

ALEX: What—they peep you?!

JESSE: Not my face.

ALEX: What?! They follow you?!

JESSE: Yes. They're outside right now. I said give me fifteen minutes, I need to get my affairs in order. They were exceedingly gracious.

    (Alex ignores this; he is already rooting through Jesse's bag.)

ALEX: Man, this is a mess—

JESSE: I was rushed, you assfuck.

ALEX: You don't think I'm being rushed? You think I appreciate this rate of turnaround? This is important.

JESSE: Why?

> (Alex doesn't respond; he is examining what is in the bag. Pulls out a piece of bone, blood and clothes hanging from it.)

JESSE: Alex. Why is this so important? Alex?!

ALEX: I don't know, do *you* like having checkpoints to go buy fucking milk?

JESSE: Yeah, but our target this time, why we going so apeshit?

ALEX: No more apeshit than normal. Shit, short arms—

> (He has shaken off the blood and clothes from the piece and is now rooting through the bag again.)

JESSE: Alex.

ALEX: Seriously? . . . Look, if we miss the player now, it's a whole 'nother month, a whole month more before this fucker comes through, at least. He's already changing his schedule up, he wasn't supposed to be through till next week. I don't want to wait another thirty. So it's a rush.

JESSE: But why this one. Who is this player we have to . . .

ALEX: To what?

JESSE: Is he *the* guy, I mean—

ALEX: I don't know. He could be. How many times we been in this room, Jesse . . . why's *this* different—

JESSE: You tell me.

> (Alex takes a step toward her.)

ALEX: Jesse, come on—

> (Jesse shies away.)

JESSE: I hate this room.

ALEX: So do I.

JESSE: Nahh, I think you like it here. I think you preference being all . . . shut away.

ALEX: It is nice being able to get something done.

JESSE: You like this.

ALEX: Why don't you start on the wires, we can double-time this. If you're really good, I'll let you run the wires into the toes.

> (Alex goes to the bag that was already in the room. He puts on latex gloves and gets out an industrial-strength black garbage bag. Beat.)

JESSE: You wanna know where it came from?

ALEX: What, the skin? Lemme guess, a cleanup guy.

JESSE: Yeah. Nice.

ALEX: Civilian?

JESSE: More or less.

ALEX: He was alone? Sloppy, sloppy cleanup guy.

JESSE: It was just a second. That part I did good. He went behind a building, just to check on strays. I was behind a dumpster. I saw his ankle. I TCB'd. I could hear his cohorts discussing his absence.

ALEX: They never follow up if someone's gone missing.

JESSE: They've started to.

ALEX: Why?

(Alex has reached into Jesse's bag. He pulls out another hunk of bone, puts it in a garbage bag. He continues taking these things out throughout the following.)

JESSE: Why do you think?

ALEX: What's their lookout? They shouldn't have let him go back alone.

JESSE: They didn't like him. I heard them say. But I thought maybe. So I started rushing. That's where mistakes were made. Then they left and I could slow down a bit. But still. Hate being exposed like that too long.

ALEX: You did good, Jesse. I'm sorry if I . . . don't think I don't . . . that you're not—this is recognized.

JESSE: Recognized.

ALEX: Yeah. What you do. You're the best and everybody knows it.

JESSE: Yeah, who everybody?

ALEX: Me. Doyle. And Doyle's who you want to recognize you.

JESSE: Uh-huh. And what occurs with this recognition?

ALEX: I'm sorry?

JESSE: What exists on the other side of being seen? 'Cuz I really'd dig that sweet corner office.

ALEX: That's not—we both know that is not what this is about.

JESSE: Then what's it about?

ALEX: They killed your parents. What else is there?

JESSE: *(Quietly.)* Everybody's a parent.

ALEX: What?

JESSE: I said . . .

(She goes to her bag. Roots through.)

ALEX: I have a system . . .

(Jesse pulls out a wedding ring.)

JESSE: He was a father. In his wallet, photos. Children. Two boys, one girl, swing set. Picture of wife, looking tired, needs work on hair. They're always parents.

ALEX: You know the rules. No personal effects.

JESSE: So they're not a person for you?

ALEX: Scavengers need to get their taste. You know that! Look, start on the

wires, get us out of here sooner; you want me to make it an order? I can
make it an order.

JESSE: Why is this important?

ALEX: I told you, a big player is coming through, like *tomorrow*, thank God
our guy on the inside—

JESSE: He's dead.

ALEX: Dead who's dead?

JESSE: Our guy. Mike. He's dead.

ALEX: How . . . how do you know he . . .

JESSE: I saw Doyle.

ALEX: You saw Doyle?

JESSE: Did you know his name? Our guy on the in?

ALEX: No, I never met—

JESSE: Yeah you did. Once.

ALEX: I'm sorry, I—

JESSE: With me. At my parents' funeral.

ALEX: The skinny kid.

JESSE: He was wiry.

ALEX: You were friends.

JESSE: We were friends.

ALEX: Good friends?

JESSE: The very fucking best.

ALEX: I'm sorry. Really. I am. But this is—

JESSE: I know what this is. I heard all about it from you. And so did Mike.

ALEX: I didn't kill him.

JESSE: Uh-huh.

ALEX: I didn't. I did not . . .

JESSE: Do you want to know how he died?

(Before Alex can really respond.)

JESSE: Machete. Did his legs first so he would bleed for longer and be in more
pain. Then they pinned his mouth open so he couldn't really scream and
his mouth went completely dry.

ALEX: Jesse—

JESSE: Then did the hands and then the rest of the arms.

ALEX: How do you—

JESSE: Doyle told me. It's on the web. Plus they left the torso and head in the
middle of the park.

ALEX: Wired to blow?

JESSE: No. They want us to see it. They want everybody to see it. It's still there, dripping in the breeze.

ALEX: They wanted to scare us—and it's working, by the looks of it.

JESSE: You don't know me very well.

ALEX: I don't?

JESSE: Not so much. Thought maybe you did.

ALEX: I know you're not scared, you don't get scared—

JESSE: I don't think you care.

ALEX: Uch. I care . . . it's just . . . this is not the moment in which I have an opportunity to care. Mike did his job and I will take time later, now I need to strain the bones, drain excess blood, tighten—

JESSE: Why we here?

ALEX: In this room?

JESSE: Yeah, this room, this skin.

ALEX: I want them gone.

JESSE: And then?

ALEX: What then?

JESSE: After they're gone. What's on the other side of this? What do we do then?

ALEX: Then we'll sort things out.

JESSE: That's it?

ALEX: No, of course not. They killed your parents, Jesse.

JESSE: I am aware! You think I am not aware?!

(Beat.)

JESSE: Why'd you work me? At the funeral?

ALEX: That was my job then.

JESSE: You went to funerals and recruited?

ALEX: Sure. Angry, sad, want revenge. Ripe.

JESSE: I was just . . . what? Meat?

ALEX: No. You were a skin. I filled you.

JESSE: Yeah. You and Doyle.

ALEX: Sure 'nuff. And you may have had some plan, but you were easy. You wanted it. I didn't remember that kid 'cuz he didn't have the same anger as you. So don't rewrite history too much yet. Wait till we win.

JESSE: 'Cuz what happens then? Streets are clear, milk on every corner, no corpses on swing sets. But then. I really need to know. What's the plan for after?

ALEX: Jesse.

JESSE: Nothing? We're just fighting now? Just turning people into skins to turn into bombs to blow up people.

ALEX: Listen. I will perform philosophy later. First the fucking skin.

(*Alex reaches into the bag again. Starts to pull out the skin, do more cleaning.*)

JESSE: Aren't you curious?

ALEX: About what?

JESSE: Where I saw Doyle?

ALEX: I assume he contacted you to meet about this.

JESSE: Without you knowing?

ALEX: Doyle doesn't need to tell me everything. I trust Doyle.

JESSE: Doyle liked Mike. He saw . . . whatever you didn't see. Maybe that's why Doyle's higher up'n you. Mike was pretty upset about him getting caught. Wanted to tell me personally.

ALEX: See what I say? He's looking out for you.

JESSE: Doyle said you miss shit sometimes.

ALEX: OK.

JESSE: Doyle said it's your limitations that—

ALEX: Can we fucking discuss Doyle said later?! I do not have time to mourn at present. Fully understood, yeah?

JESSE: (*Quietly.*) But I only have five minutes left.

ALEX: For what?!

JESSE: I need to know why we're doing this. Why is this important? What do we win?

ALEX: You want to live like this? Our streets not our own. Our world not our own.

JESSE: And we get the player coming through, that changes it. Changes things.

ALEX: Sure. A start.

JESSE: Yeah. But when does it end?

(*Beat.*)

ALEX: Right this second? I most honestly do not know.

(*Jesse takes this in. Alex keeps on working, sorting the bones from the skin.*)

JESSE: I really wish you had a better answer.

ALEX: Yeah so do I.

JESSE: Just wish you had a better—

ALEX: You want me to be honest? Or to lie to you?

JESSE: I wanted to be able to let you go.

ALEX: Let me go where? God, you're—I'm sorry about Mike. I am. Just—Jesse. Go. I'll contact you in three days, we'll debrief then . . .

JESSE: Actually, I saw Doyle twice.

ALEX: Yeah?

JESSE: Yeah. He contacted me to tell me 'bout Mike. Then I got the skin. The cleanup-crew skin. Then I contacted him.

ALEX: Doyle's busy, it's amazing he had time to see you once.

JESSE: He felt guilt. Guilt motivates. He felt bad about Mike, dying and being chopped up and etcetera.

ALEX: I am sorry.

JESSE: What Doyle said.

ALEX: We're always sorry to lose someone.

JESSE: What Doyle said too. But see after I talked to him, and I went and did the job, and got the skin, after I killed the cleanup guy behind a dumpster and was separating him best I could given circumstances and my personal state of mind, and then unfortunately peeping photo of the happy fam in the happy fam homestead, I started thinking 'bout what Doyle put out there. And what Doyle put out there is it's a tragedy Mike was found, bound, and sliced to pieces. And that we all felt bad. And I thought, how bad could I possibly feel if I'm doing this.

ALEX: It's war.

JESSE: No. It's killing. We're killing. They're killing for them. I'm killing for you and Doyle.

ALEX: No, c'mon, that's not—you're killing for everyone. We're just cogs.

JESSE: Doyle a cog?

ALEX: Big cog sure.

JESSE: Not anymore.

(Alex looks at Jesse confused.)

JESSE: You should look under the bones.

(Alex digs in the bag. Sees something. Moves away from the bag.)

ALEX: There are two skins.

JESSE: Yeah. I actually did a real good job on the first one. Amazingly good, considering circumstances and the lot. But on Doyle, I was way rushed.

ALEX: Oh my God.

JESSE: Sloppy. Sloppy sloppy Jesse.

(Alex is silent.)

JESSE: Still, two for the price of one. If you think about, this would in theory give us a better shot at the guy. Wire 'em both up, more bang, more damages . . .

ALEX: How did you—

JESSE: Guilt. I was crying. He felt bad. He hugged me. I—

(She reaches into her bag and pulls out a very sharp weapon, like some kind of miniscythe action.)

JESSE: Am seriously superfucking quick with this mothafucka. He tried to say something but the blood was in his lungs like right away. He looked sorry though.

ALEX: Oh God. Oh God.

JESSE: Can't help.

ALEX: Jesse, I—what did you do—

JESSE: He killed Mike.

ALEX: No—

JESSE: Sure. Others did it too. But I've killed beaucoup de them, yah?

ALEX: Doyle didn't make—they killed your parents—

JESSE: The cleanup guy's daughter's gonna grow up soon. And then where am I gonna be?

(Alex looks at the weapon. He is clearly calculating something.)

JESSE: Don't worry 'bout this.

(Jesse puts it down, near Alex. Walks away from it. Faces him. Alex lets it sit there a moment. Picks it up.)

ALEX: I'm not gonna kill you.

JESSE: No?

ALEX: If I do, it'll all be a mystery what really happened—you need to tell everyone.

JESSE: It's not gonna go like that.

ALEX: Yes it will.

JESSE: No. You need to kill me in the next ninety seconds.

ALEX: What?

JESSE: My fifteen minutes is almost up.

ALEX: What're you—?

JESSE: After I killed Doyle. I went to them. They were happy. I proved Doyle was dead. I promised I'd give them back the cleanup guy. I promised them you. I just asked for fifteen minutes first.

ALEX: You went to them?

JESSE: They're outside.

(Alex looks at the doors.)

JESSE: Nice of them, yeah? To wait. Patient.

ALEX: Fuck you!

JESSE: They're just at the front door. Don't know about the back. Was gonna help you get out, not tell 'em. But your answers did not pass muster, as it goes.

ALEX: You already did it.

JESSE: Not all of it. They're gonna do the knock. About sixty seconds. You know the knock. And then they'll knock the door down.

ALEX: Fuck you I'm gonna kill you!

JESSE: Please.

ALEX: What?

JESSE: Kill me. Kill me. I killed Doyle. I betrayed you. They're gonna shoot you on sight. They're gonna skin you. You may as well kill me.

ALEX: Why did you do this? You didn't have to do this!

JESSE: Once it started I didn't know how to make it stop.

(She pulls a knife out of her pocket.)

JESSE: Do you need me to make you defend yourself? Or could you just TCB?

ALEX: Aren't they gonna kill you too?

JESSE: Not if they can help it. I helped them. Now they can use me.

ALEX: And you trust them?

JESSE: Why do you think I wanna die?

ALEX: I should . . .

JESSE: Kill me. Kill me. *(He takes a step toward her.)*

ALEX: No. I should make you live with this. Shouldn't I?

(Three tremendous pounds at the door. Beat. Blackout.)

END OF PLAY

Specter (or, Broken Down by Age & Sex)

NEENA BEBER

Originally commissioned and produced by the
stageFARM, at Cherry Lane Theatre, New York City,
October 4–December 1, 2007, as part of Vengeance,
a series of short plays. Directed by Alex Kilgore.
Cast: Phil—David Wilson Barnes; Lana—Lisa Joyce.

CHARACTERS

PHIL, a famous man in a strange wig, well past his prime; he is charismatic and a little creepy.

LANA, a blond actress who looks like she could be twenty-five but might be pushing forty, still hoping for her big break; she is a looker with a steely sweetness and a genuine, wholesome quality.

SETTING

The foyer of Phil Spector's house.

TIME

The play is loosely based on actual events that took place on the last night of Lana Clarkson's life (February 3, 2003), and for which Spector, originator of the so-called Wall of Sound, would soon stand trial.

• • •

Phil Spector's foyer. Lana is in the bathroom, offstage.

PHIL: What I like about you

what I love about you and note how I'm not afraid of using the word "love"—

I'm not one of those men who shies away from the word "love," no, I'm all about love.

I practically invented love, as a brandable concept anyway, Lord knows I made quite a few buckets of cold hard cash because I understand and feel and create love and give love and accept love and what I love about you is not just your beauty—

(The toilet flushes.)

PHIL: As I was saying.

Though there is that, Lord knows,

and I am not afraid of beauty

I believe in beauty

yes it's a religion for me

Beauty

God is beauty

You are God then, ha ha, you see what I mean

you see your power over me

over the world

with your beauty and what I love

about you

about YOU, yes

is your

absolute balls-out up-for-anything up-for-life questing searching acting

spontaneity

you are game

am I right

you are fucking game.

LANA: *(Entering from the bathroom.)* I am so fucking game.

PHIL: Say that again, darlin'.

LANA: I'm game.

PHIL: No, not that part. The other part.

LANA: What part?

PHIL: "Fucking." Say "fucking."

Do you know what a turn-on that is

a beautiful mouth emitting foul words

luscious lips surrounding

Words

fuck cunt dick pussy fuck

LANA: I'm game because I'm loving and fun but I'm not that game, OK?

PHIL: I get that.

People are complicated, you're complicated.

People are deep, you're . . .

No, that's not true, people are shallow. Women are fucking shallow.

But you're deep.

You

are deep.

LANA: Thank you, Phil.

And you know what, Phil?

I also believe in love. I also believe in beauty.

So that's, like, really cool that we've really connected in this way.

That's cool.

But I'm going to have to go now, OK?

PHIL: Not OK.

(Phil wanders around to pour more drinks. He's already drunk. Lana might be getting ready to go, putting her purse on her shoulder.)

PHIL: *(Singing.)* Well there's snakes on the mountain,

And eels in the sea,

'Twas a red-headed woman
Made a wreck out of me,
An' it looks like
I'm never gonna cease my wanderin'.
If the whiskey don't get you,
Then the women must . . .
(Spoken.)
Did I say red-headed woman? I meant a blond . . .
a beautiful blondorini . . .
(Phil finishes the pouring, presents her with the drink.)

LANA: *(About the song.)* Is that one of yours?

PHIL: No. Always liked it, though. Reminds me of my daddy.

LANA: He played it?

PHIL: Never. Reminds me of him, though. Anonymous fucking genius anony-
    mous wrote it. Anonymous is my toughest competition.
    (He hands her a drink.)

LANA: Oh, no more for me, thanks.

PHIL: Another soda pop then? Coca Cola?
    I can see about you
    that you're not just another
    face. You're
    more
    than a face.

LANA: Thanks.

PHIL: You're also a body. Ha ha. No.
    Seriously, sweetheart . . .

LANA: So the driver . . . Should I . . .

PHIL: You're not—

LANA: . . . let him know I'm . . .

PHIL: Not going.

LANA: ready. I'm ready.

PHIL: Not yet.

LANA: What?

PHIL: No.

LANA: But—

PHIL: One more.
    *(He stops her a little aggressively. He downs his drink as Lana tries to wait
    patiently, but there's awkwardness. She looks around, ready to go.)*

LANA: This castle reminds me of

when I was little

you know

Sleeping Beauty,

fairy tales . . .

PHIL: Beauty and the Beast.

LANA: Well, yeah.

PHIL: Is this your first time inside a real castle? It was worth the drive, right?

I wanted you to see

a real

fucking

I always knew I'd reside in

a fucking

castle

have you ever in your life . . .

so am I your first? Castle?

LANA: Oh, no, Phil, I actually swept cinders in a castle.

I was Cinderella in our senior play in high school. And you know what?

I rocked that cardboard castle. I made it real.

PHIL: You're funny. You have humor.

A beautiful woman is not often funny and here you are,

On top of everything else,

funny.

LANA: Making people laugh is my forte. That's what I discovered about myself.

And you know I wish I'd had one on me, what I want you to see, what I really want you to see I just know you're going to love it, is this tape I made, of my show, of me, but not just me because it's me doing my characters and they are all so funny and so real to me, you should see my Little Richard,

I am definitely going to send you that tape of me

doing my characters

you are going to really like it, Phil.

I woke up one day, I woke up and said to myself, "Lana, what do you love to do?" "You, Lana, you love to make people laugh," I said to myself, Lana, and Lana does make people laugh, her skills as a comedienne are really her best skills.

Others have said. So that might surprise you. About me.

PHIL: You're a gem, Laura.

LANA: Lana.

PHIL: Even better.

    A movie star name.

    Well of course you are a movie star

LANA: Thank you for that acknowledgment, Phil.

    I have a lot of red carpets to walk down that I haven't walked down yet, but I have walked down a few.

PHIL: Now that could be a song, "I have a lot of red carpets to walk on down."

    I could work with that. C&W folk pop with an operatic . . .

    twang.

    If Lennon were alive I'd get him to do it. We were like brothers, you know, me an' Lennon

    John Lennon

    brothers . . .

    I'm going to make some calls

    maybe Bob

    Bob could use a

    light touch

    a . . .

LANA: A Lana touch!

PHIL: That's right.

    And Sam would've . . . and Joey . . . but you know a lot of them, they're . . .

    so many dead

    you know

    it happens

    it's important to find the ones

    who are living

    let's get out song to Bob before he isn't, what do you say?

    Bob's a . . . friend of mine . . . Dylan.

LANA: Me, a songwriter! I love it! Let's do it!

    I've been writing, that's really more and more my thing, the words, the words coming from inside me, you know.

    I like to generate

    my own material

    my own life.

    I haven' been lucky the last few years but I am a lucky person, I just need to change my luck.

PHIL: You're here. Blam. It's happening. I can help you. Do you sing?

LANA: Yes. Not exactly. But I can sell a song.

I can sell a song like nobody's business.

PHIL: Nobody's business, that's a hook, I can work with that.

Yeah, you can sell anything in my book, Lady.

LANA: Lana.

PHIL: You could get discovered today. Tonight. Tomorrow. This morning.

What the fuck time is it?

People get discovered. They are found. They are made.

You could pull me out of retirement, not retirement seclusion, exile,

whatever it is I'm,

wherever I am . . .

you could pull me out in any case

with your face that sank a thousand . . .

LANA: I suspected

there was a reason

for us to meet and you see I'm sorry I didn't know

who you were, had no idea, "treat him like gold,"

they said, and is it possible, Phil, that you are my pot of gold at the end

of my rainbow? And I'm yours?

Of course you've had a lot of pots of gold so to speak, but I could be

your next one!

Because there's gold in me, Phil, I know there is.

Discovery. Like that. Snap your fingers.

That hasn't been my path but I think it's better this way

that I have to work harder than most

to make use of my God-given gifts

and share them—

(He puts a hand on her breast.)

What are you doing?

PHIL: You're lovely.

LANA: *(Removing his hand.) Philip . . . ? Philip now, now now . . .*

PHIL: I've got four hundred stitches in the back of my head,

did you know that?

I almost died. Went flying though a windshield. In fact I was dead.

I came back because there are goddesses on earth.

Between God and goddesses, is that a hard choice?

That is not a hard choice.

You're divine.

(He puts his hand on her breast again.)
LANA: *(Removing his hand again.)* OK, thank you.
 (He puts his hands in his pants.)
PHIL: Come upstairs.
LANA: I have to go home now, Philip. I have to sleep.
PHIL: Nobody leaves the fucking castle
 until I say.
 You do not leave.
 You stay.
LANA: I have an audition.
 It's a good one, a really good one.
 I'm perfect for it.
 I check the breakdowns every day.
 You have to do that.
 Take care of yourself.
 Not rely on others.
 You need to remind them. You need to pester.
 I need to go home, get some sleep, a fresh start,
 memorize my lines.
PHIL: We don't have to sleep together tonight.
 We don't have to sleep at all.
 Who needs sleep. Fuck sleep. Sleep is a thief.
 It's the opposite of life.
 Upstairs is a view of the sunrise not to be missed.
LANA: You said one drink. That's what I agreed to. One. Thank you for the
 drink. I have to go now, Mr. Spector.
 It's been an honor.
 I'm going to send you my characters, my tape, you're going to love it,
 OK?
 (He takes a gun out of a drawer.)
PHIL: A .38 blue steel Colt with a two-inch barrel. One of my favorites. Want
 to take a closer look?
LANA: I'm not really comfortable? Around guns? I'm sorry, I really need to go,
 I need to get out of here, it's late, too late—
 (Phil pulls the gun on Lana. She screams. They struggle.)
PHIL: You are not going. Did I not make myself clear?
 Was I somehow not clear?
 Every woman deserves to have her fucking brains blown out of her head,
 by the by. Every woman.

(Getting gun inside her mouth.)

Every fucking cunt.

(Lights shift. Reality breaks. Vaudeville or Borscht Belt. Lana steps forward.)

LANA: *(As Jewish mother.)* Harvey Philip. Why do you talk that way? Such a mouth on you young people these days.

PHIL: Shut up, Ma. You don't know what you're talking about.

LANA: *(As Jewish mother.) Harvey Phillip. Look what I brought you today. A tuna sandwich, just how you like it. With a hard-boiled egg and extra mayo. For the protein. You're not eating right, Harvey Phillip. You're too skinny, Harvey Phillip. I don't care how these big famous rock and roll types of people like to look, you need some fat on your bones!*

PHIL: Christ, now I see how you killed Dad. You drove him there. Drove him to suicide with your endless bitching and nagging and chicken fat in his face.

LANA: *(As Jewish mother.) Eat the tuna right now I came all the way down here eat it Harvey Phillip I know what's good for you Mama knows best eat it!*

PHIL: I fucking hate rye bread. You know I hate rye bread. You're fucking in my face with the fucking rye bread all the time, fuck off!

LANA: *(As Jewish mother.) Pumpernickel, I thought you hated pumpernickel. You love rye.*

PHIL: It's soul murder in the guise of kindness. Lay off! You killed Dad and now you're killing me!

LANA: *(As Jewish mother.) Always blame the mother. And if the mother is Jewish? Fuggedaboudit, it's on Mama, overbearing, smothering Mama. Blame the love of the Jewish mama for everything wrong in the world, why don't you! Feh!*

(The skit is over. Sound of applause as Lana takes a bow.)

LANA: Thank you. Eventually, if you refuse to give up, give up on your dreams, then eventually you will have your chance at luck. I believe.

PHIL: Shut up already. Shut up. Do you have any idea what's it's like to carry the weight of a woman like that sitting on your soul day in and day fucking out?

LANA: *(As crazy sister.)* She was my mother, too. And who killed Mother? You, Phil. You. You did it.

PHIL: If only I'd had the chance!

LANA: You did it with your words, Mr. H. P. Spector, Mr. Big Shot, mouthing off to some so-called fancy biographer of your so-called fancy-ass self so you could get *your* story out there, so *you* could be the one, the one with a story. What about me? What about my story? What about Mother's story? Your so-called revelations are what put Mother in the grave and me in the kookoo-bin.

PHIL: *(Calmly.)* You were already in the koo-koo bin. And Mother didn't die. Not then and not for years.

LANA: *(As crazy sister.)* You killed me and I'm still alive. I was going to be a movie star. I was going to have a story. I was going to be the one. Mother moved to Hollywood for me. For me. You're a Bronx boy. You'll always be a Bronx boy. Hollywood was my deal. But you sucked the air out of my dreams, you took over my life, you took everything, Harvey Phillip, you took it all for yourself, you greedy filthy disgusting piiiig.

(Taking bow.) Thank you, thank you.

PHIL: A .38 Colt is D minor. That pop. D minor. I have perfect pitch. Your voice is in the key of A.

(Beat; he is listening to notes inside his head that no one else hears.)

Perfect pitch is the ability to identify the exact key and tones of isolated auditory stimuli on the basis of pitch alone without external reference. Everything is music to me.

The death of my father by carbon monoxide poisoning was completely silent. Silent.

A gun has music.

He had no music.

There was the F-flat screeching ranting braying of my mother and my sister

or the silence of sleep.

I needed to make music

my own.

To find voices

for my notes.

LANA: *(As Ronnie Spector.)* I don't do regrets. And I don't do bitter.

PHIL: Some people are going to find that offensive. Your impersonation of a person.

LANA: *(As Ronnie Spector.)* Look in the mirror, babe. Ain't no wig on earth gonna make you human.

PHIL: You will not leave me. Not now. Not ever. You are nothing without me. I made you. I created you. B minor. A haunting quality. Vulnerable but raunchy, too. Sweet and trashy. My sound. Be my baby. MY baby. Sing it. Fucking sing it.

LANA: *(As Ronnie Spector.)* I ain't gonna sing for you 'cause you'd steal that from me, too, if you could. I'm gonna get back up on that stage someday, away from you, baby, away from this prison you've locked me in, I'm gonna get up on that stage, alone, me and my voice, and be happy . . . You got it all, baby. But what makes me happy? This. Inside me. You can't get my voice. You lose. *(Twirling a bow.)* Thank you . . .

PHIL: I don't lose. I never lose.

I WIN!!!

(Phil goes back to the chair, gun in hand. Lana puts her blond Lana wig back on and heads back up to the chair during the following.)

LANA: Sometimes I feel like I'm playing a part. And it's not a part I would have gone out for. I don't think I'm right for it, for the part I got cast in, at all. For one thing I'm just too young for my age, don't you think? And it's so B movie, and now somebody else has the option on my life. Someone else's clothes. Someone else's hairdo. Someone else's body. And a soul; I think it's my soul, but . . . I'm not sure. Because somehow, I can't help feeling that this just isn't the part I was meant to play. Not at all.

(Beat.)

LANA: *(Taking her seat.)* I spent many years in situations in which I had to forgive myself. So I believe in forgiveness. I do. And I believe in love. I still do. I just do.

(Lana places her hands on the gun as Phil, shaky, holds it.)

I came here tonight to change my luck.

Because you never know, right?

(The gun is back in her mouth. The Wall of Sound sound comes up.)

PHIL: The sound of a bullet blasting through brains, a woman's brains, carries with it its own symphonic resonance. It should be supported with strings, a whole section of strings, and with wind, of course. Trumpets, saxophone, French horn, and trombone. The clarinet comes after.

I see a C and D chord, heavy on mandolin and violin, underneath a simple steady drumbeat, and then the lush build to full.

Note that the breath may persist after cessation of heartbeat.

The breath.

The last breath.

If your last breath was in, after death, there will still be out.

(Orchestrating and arranging the moment.)

A symphony of breath, agonal breaths, a dying gasp in the key of B, fade out drums, and then . . .

(Wall of Sound music fades out.)

LANA: I love the canals in Venice.

Not the famous Italian Venice, though I'd love to go there, too.

The famous Californian Venice. It was built to be a perfect copy of the original. I like that somehow. A perfect copy. It isn't, of course. It's its own thing. I like that too. I like a view of water. It may not be much, but it's my view. And the thing about a canal is, it looks like it would be so easy to cross. You don't even have to know how to swim that well. You can just do it. Leap across, almost. It looks like you almost could. And all of my dreams are so big, it's nice to have a little one like that. Just kind of, flying across that little strip of water.

PHIL: *(Still hearing his own symphony, producing it.)* Shhh. . . . Shhh . . .

I was going to be a court reporter because I like to listen and to record. I liked the sound of the clackety-clack.

But it was too graphic. The words.

Those aren't the kinds of words I like.

Too specific.

I'm abstract.

That's the thing about me.

The thing no one seems to really get

about me.

LANA: I think in my dreams I leave my body.

But, like, I love my body.

And the thing about leaving my body is, where would I even go?

PHIL: Your luck is about to change.

LANA: Is it?

PHIL: Your luck is about to change.

LANA: It has to.

PHIL: Your luck and my luck, one of us is meant to get lucky tonight, tell me who, who's going to get lucky, who?

LANA: I think our luck is intertwined from here on. What if it is?

PHIL: *(Can't stop from pulling the trigger.)* Fuck.

(Blackout and gun shot simultaneous. Music up.)

END OF PLAY

That Thing

JOHN SHANAHAN

Originally performed in the Boston Theater Marathon,
May 20, 2007. Produced by Image Theater, Lowell,
Massachusetts. Directed by Fran Weinberg.
Cast: Linda Edgerton—Kippy Goldfarb;
Carl Edgerton—Dale Place.

    CARL EDGERTON, late sixties.
    LINDA EDGERTON, late sixties.

SETTING
    The porch of a house.

TIME
    The present: Sunday morning.

• • •

At rise: Two chairs at center, a small table between them. Carl and Linda are sharing their usual quiet Sunday morning sitting on the porch. He's poring over a crossword puzzle; she's busy knitting or crocheting. After a few beats, Carl chuckles to himself, a big smile on his face.

LINDA: What?

CARL: Oh, nothing. *(He looks at her and chuckles again.)*

LINDA: *What?*

CARL: I was just thinking about that thing we used to do.

LINDA: What thing?

CARL: You know. The *thing.*

LINDA: I have no idea what you're talking about.

CARL: Yes, you do! You know, the thing we did sometimes. The thing with the, the . . . *(He makes an odd, strangely complicated but meaningless gesture with his hands.)* the other thing.

LINDA: Oh . . . *that. (She returns to her yarn.)*

CARL: *(With an obscene chuckle.)* Yeah . . . *that.* Heh, heh. Hadn't thought of that one in quite a while. Hoo boy! You remember now, don't you?

LINDA: Yes.

CARL: I figured you would. Oh, I figured you would!

LINDA: Yes. Never cared much for that.

CARL: What?

LINDA: *(Plainly.)* I never liked it.

CARL: You did, too.

LINDA: No, I really didn't.

CARL: I was *there*, Linda. I know you liked it.

LINDA: Honestly, dear, I didn't.

CARL: Never?

LINDA: *(Looks up, thinking a moment.)* No. Never.

CARL: But you did it! A couple of times, even!

LINDA: Well, of course I did, dear. That doesn't mean I enjoyed it.

CARL: Then why did you do it?

LINDA: Because you enjoyed it.

CARL: And that's the only reason?

LINDA: *(Chuckling.)* I don't think there *is* another reason to do something like that, Carl.

CARL: But you did.

LINDA: *(Reaching over to pat his leg.)* Yes, I did, dear.

CARL: But you didn't like it.

LINDA: No.

CARL: I did.

LINDA: I know.

> *(Pause.)*

CARL: I don't believe you.

LINDA: That's fine, dear.

CARL: Because it was good.

LINDA: For you.

CARL: And you.

LINDA: No.

CARL: No?

LINDA: No.

CARL: Why not?

LINDA: Why wasn't it good for me?

CARL: Yes.

LINDA: Because I didn't like it.

CARL: But why didn't you like it?

LINDA: I just didn't. A person can't like everything, now can they?

CARL: *(Uncertainly.)* No. No, I . . . I guess . . . not.

> *(Pause. Linda knits. Carl's working through the illogical conclusion he's about to come to. It's not pleasing him, and it starts to show on his face.)*

CARL: So what else didn't you like?

LINDA: How's that?

CARL: If a person can't like everything, then what else didn't you like?

LINDA: *(Trying for humor.)* I was never very big on cauliflower.

CARL: You know what I mean!

LINDA: Oh, Carl . . .

CARL: No, no, don't "oh, Carl" me! Tell me! If you didn't like the *(He makes hand gesture.)* thing, then what else didn't you like?

LINDA: It was all quite fine, dear.

CARL: Fi—Fine? *Fine?*

LINDA: Yes. Fine.

CARL: That's all? Just "fine"?

LINDA: What's wrong with fine?

CARL: What's wrong with . . . ? I'll tell you what's wrong with fine! What's wrong with fine is that it's *fine*. It's not great, it's not good, it's not even OK, it's *fine.*

LINDA: Fine and OK are the same thing, dear.

CARL: Aha! See? There! You said it yourself. Not great, not good—

LINDA: You're making entirely too much out of this, Carl.

CARL: No, I don't think I am! Thirty-seven years of marriage and it's just now that I find out you didn't like having sex with me?

LINDA: I never said that!

CARL: You might just as well have!

LINDA: I said nothing of the sort!

CARL: You said it was fine.

LINDA: And it was!

CARL: There you go again!

LINDA: Oh, Carl.

CARL: And again with the "oh, Carl"!

LINDA: You're being ridiculous. You know that, don't you?

CARL: I have every right to be ridiculous! *(Pause, as he realizes that came out wrong.)* I have every right to be upset about this.

LINDA: There's nothing to be upset about, dear.

CARL: And that "dear" thing—don't think even for a minute that I don't know that any time you say "dear" you're just trying to humor me.

LINDA: That is not true!

CARL: Oh, yes it is! I know it is.

LINDA: If you say so . . . *(She realizes she was about to say "dear.")*

CARL: Ha! You see? You were going to say it again! So humor me, Linda, why don't you? What else didn't you like? Huh? Come on! Tell me! *(Pause. She won't look him in the eye. She fidgets a bit.)*

CARL: See! I knew there was something! What is it?

LINDA: Oh, Carl . . .

CARL: Come on.

LINDA: I don't want to get into this.

CARL: Yeah? Well, I do . . . *dear.*

LINDA: Do you, now?

CARL: Damn right I do.

LINDA: *(With a sigh.)* If you must know, I always thought you tended to . . . dawdle a bit.

CARL: "Dawdle"?

LINDA: Yes.

CARL: What the hell does "dawdle" mean?

LINDA: There were times when you . . . well, you just . . . *(Sighs.)* You had a tendency to stay too long in one place when you really ought to have been getting on with it. OK?

(Carl tries to take this in for a moment. It's just not registering.)

CARL: Too long? It's called foreplay, Linda.

LINDA: I'm familiar with the term, thank you.

CARL: And if you wanted me to "get on with it," you could have said something!

LINDA: Well, I didn't want to be rude! You always seemed to be enjoying yourself!

CARL: It's a good thing one of us was!

LINDA: Carl . . .

CARL: Isn't this just great? Thirty-seven years and you never said anything! So is that it? Huh? Is it just that I "dawdled"? Anything else I was doing wrong, huh?

LINDA: It wasn't "wrong," Carl, it's just that sometimes it wasn't what I would have preferred.

CARL: Well, then you should have said something, Linda. You know? You should have said something.

LINDA: Really, now?

CARL: Yeah, really.

LINDA: Huh.

(She turns back to her knitting. He huffs and smirks like he's won and picks his crossword back up. Quiet moments pass.)

LINDA: There could have been more.

CARL: What?

LINDA: There could have been more.

CARL: More things you didn't like?

LINDA: No. *More.* More often, and when you did get around to it, there could have been . . . you know . . . more.

CARL: More? You got plenty!

LINDA: Did I?

CARL: Damn right you did!

LINDA: Seems to me that if I had, I wouldn't be thinking there could have been more, now would I?

CARL: I never heard any complaints!

LINDA: Yes, well, it's a little hard to hear when you're asleep, dear.

(Carl's aghast—can't speak.)

LINDA: *(With a chuckle.)* One and done! *(Pats his leg.)* That's my Carl!

CARL: Whuh—huh—I—buh . . .

LINDA: And while I'm thinking of it, Carl, you might like to know that you can't get me in the mood by smacking me on the butt and saying, "How about it, baby?"

CARL: *(Like a weak, defeated defense.)* Sometimes I bought flowers.

LINDA: Of course you did, dear.

CARL: *(Distant and a little sad.)* You never liked it.

LINDA: Carl, I liked it. Of course I liked it. It was me and the only man I've ever loved, making love. And that's beautiful. But you wanted me to be honest, and there were things I just wasn't crazy about.

CARL: Well, you know, there were some things you did that I didn't like so much.

LINDA: No, there weren't.

CARL: Oh-ho yes, there were.

LINDA: Name one.

(He's busted. She called his bluff, and his face shows it.)

LINDA: And there you are.

(Pause. They look at each other. He sighs. She smiles. He takes up his puzzle. She's still watching him.)

LINDA: How long do you figure it's been?

CARL: How's that?

LINDA: I think it's been a while.

CARL: Um . . . true, now that you mention it.

LINDA: *(Like a verbal blush.)* I sort of liked talking about it.

CARL: Oh. Well . . . good.

LINDA: No, Carl, I really *liked* talking about it. I think we're done talking about it.

(He's a little confused, but then she smiles very broadly, and he gets it. School-boy excitement takes over—he's both thrilled and flustered!)

CARL: Oh! Oh-ho! Well! OK, then! Yes! So, uh . . . I don't have any flowers.

LINDA: You don't need them.

CARL: No. OK. No flowers. Could I—do I—wine! Wine? Do you want wine?

LINDA: That would be nice. Thank you.

CARL: OK! I can do that! Wine! Right! Kitchen! I should . . . I . . .

LINDA: Why don't you get the wine and wait for me upstairs?

CARL: Upstairs! Yes! OK! Good! Get the wine, go upstairs. Upstairs is good. I like upstairs. Upstairs!

(He starts to head off.)

LINDA: Carl?

(He snaps to a stop.)

CARL: Yeah!

LINDA: I was wondering. Do, um . . . do we still have the . . . *(She makes the hand gesture.)*

CARL: I think so. Maybe?

LINDA: We may not need it, but how about if you go look for it?

(He smiles like it's Christmas.)

CARL: I will! Oh, I will!

(He grabs her face and kisses her, then all but runs off, perhaps with a little "woo hoo!" Linda stands up, smiling and pleased with herself. She takes a few moments and primps a bit.)

CARL: *(Off.)* Linda! Are you coming?

LINDA: *(Calling.)* I'll be right there! *(A beat then, almost to herself, smiling.) Dear. (She struts off the stage like a lady who's about to get some good lovin'. The lights fade.)*

END OF PLAY

Tongue, Tied

M. Thomas Cooper

Presented by Actors Theatre of Louisville in conjunction with
the 32nd Annual Humana Festival of New American Plays,
Actors Theatre, Louisville, Kentucky, March 2008.
Directed by Marc Masterson. Cast: Tina—Emily Ackerman;
Tom—Stephen Plunkett.

CHARACTERS

TINA, a young woman with different colored socks on each hand. Her
socks are Jean-Claude (left hand) and Latisha (right hand).

TOM, a young man with different colored socks on each hand. His socks
are Mr. Chan (left hand) and Sven (right hand).

SETTING

A psychiatrist's waiting room.

TIME

The present.

NOTE: A slash (/) indicates that the next character begins to speak his or her
line, overlapping the first speaker.

•   •   •

*Tina sits, hands hidden behind her, waiting. After a moment her right hand
jumps.*

TINA: Stop it. *(Again her right hand jumps.)* I said, STOP IT.
(Again her right hand jumps.) Latisha! Damn it! I said, STOP! *(Tina begins struggling to keep her right hand behind her.)* No . . . no . . . . I said
. . . NO. No-no-no-no no-no. Latisha . . . ! *(Tina's right hand, Latisha,
bolts out and looks around.)*

LATISHA: Girl, how many times have I told you? You gotta stop keepin' us down
like that. Look at this bright, crazy world you're trying to keep us from.
Just look at it! Ain't it amazin'?!

TINA: Latisha, you know I'm not trying to keep you down. I'm attempting to
live an ordinary and relatively content life.

LATISHA: Ain't we all, sista. Ain't we all.

TINA: And having a black woman, who happens . . . .

LATISHA: A proud, powerful woman of color. Thank you.

TINA: Exactly. A proud, powerful woman of color, who happens to be a sock,
living on my hand . . .

LATISHA: Hey, you can't just blame me. I thought there was also some hot, little piece of French crème brûlée dancin' on your other mitten? *(A slight
pause as Tina fights with her left hand.)* Ain't that right?
(More struggling and then Tina's left hand, Jean-Claude, bursts forth.)

JEAN-CLAUDE: Bien sur! Parceque we will revolt and lop your pretty bourgeois head off!

LATISHA: Jean-Claude, why do you always opt for overdramatic reactionism, when intelligent discourse can . . .

JEAN-CLAUDE: Latisha, you and your intelligent discourse can suck my left . . .

TINA: People, people, people . . . please! Can we not simply sit here and get along? Isn't that what I've been attempting? To coordinate vast and diametrically opposed perspectives since I acquired you two.

JEAN-CLAUDE: Acquired? More like forced encampment.

LATISHA: Yeah, acquired, my big, beautiful ass. If I remember right, some dude named Matt dumped your skinny rump and you were all—

JEAN-CLAUDE: Oh, boo-hoo. Oh, boo-hoo. Look at me I'm all alone.

LATISHA: No one loves me. I wish I weren't soooo forlorn. Soooo despondent, dejected, and alone.

TINA: I didn't say—

JEAN-CLAUDE: Mon cher, I'm afraid you did. And voilà, we is ici.

LATISHA: That's right. We're here and there's no way you can blame us.

TINA: Yes, well . . . It might be different if you two didn't bicker and argue so much. I might be able to enjoy your company. However . . .
(Tom enters. His hands are thrust deep in his jacket pockets. Tina hides her hands behind her. Tom sits. A long, long uncomfortable silence. A few twitches from both their respective backs and pockets.)

TINA: Can you believe how hot it is?

TOM: I know. Why just the other day I could swear I saw a dog / burst into flames. A dog didn't actually catch fire . . .

TINA: It seems like it's a million degrees out there. I don't really mean a million degrees,

TINA/TOM: That'd be crazy.
(Tina and Tom struggle to keep their hands hidden, however, to no avail. Simultaneously, Latisha, Jean-Claude, Mr. Chan, and Sven leap out.)

SVEN: Tom, if I'm not mistaken, keeping any part of your consciousness purposefully in the dark, regardless how unwanted, is perhaps not the best coping mechanism.

MR. CHAN: I've no idea what he just said, but I will agree with it.

JEAN-CLAUDE: Mademoiselle, what'd I say about your bourgeois head?

LATISHA: Girl, are you not thinkin'? Keep this up I'll help the little Frenchie.

JEAN-CLAUDE: Little? Moi? I'll have you know my nickname is Mont Blanc.

SVEN: Mont Blanc?

LATISHA: And who is this cutie? Hello.

(Tina and Tom shove their hands away.)

TOM: My father was a magician in the Tibetan army during the occupation of New Zealand in 1972.

TINA: I'm an entertainer. My show is in Vegas.

TOM: Every night he would entertain the troops with magic and vaudeville.

TINA: I inherited my act from a crazy, one-legged aunt who raised me after my parents were devoured by bunnies on a Tuesday during a solar eclipse.

TOM: Then during the month the natives call Rama-rama, a witch doctor cast a spell on his socks.

TINA: My one-legged aunt was very strict and hated fingerprints on anything, thus I became conditioned to wear socks on my hands.

TOM: The next morning Sven and Mr. Chan had arrived—invariably I have inherited the curse.

TINA/TOM: Honestly, I'm not crazy.

(Beat. Gradually Latisha, Jean-Claude, Sven, and Mr. Chan slip out of the shadows.)

TINA: I'm . . . I'm Tina.

TOM: Hello. I'm Tom.

JEAN-CLAUDE: And I'm a turtledove.

MR. CHAN: Tom, if you want, I'll kick his ass. Now.

SVEN: Violence is the first choice of the ignorant.

MR. CHAN: And after french-frying Frenchie, I'll teach Sven about the philosophy of the fist.

JEAN-CLAUDE: From a hospital bed. Prepare to be Jean-Clobbered.

LATISHA: Is that Tom with one M, or two?

TOM: Just . . . just one.

LATISHA: Ain't goin' ta do. Don't you know the ladies like things double-sized?

TINA: Latisha! I thought we agreed you wouldn't . . .

TOM: Well, I . . . I guess I'm willing to add a letter . . .

JEAN-CLAUDE: Ah, what a pansy, he'll change anything—even his name—at the drop of a hat.

TOM: No, but for the right woman I'm willing to . . .

JEAN-CLAUDE: Boo! Now you can change your panties, too. Hahahahahaha!

MR. CHAN: Let me kick his ass. Let me beat that French smirk off his . . .

TOM: Mr. Chan, no. No. Remember the song? The song, Mr. Chan . . . the song . . . War?

MR. CHAN: War? What's it good for?

TOM: Absolutely nothing.

JEAN-CLAUDE: Singing, little pansy, I would make pâté out of you.

SVEN: Ignore him, Mr. Chan. His anger and frustration is from not having found love.

LATISHA: I knew there was a reason I liked you. War?! What's it good for?

MR. CHAN: Absolutely nothing!

LATISHA: Say it again!

MR. CHAN: Absolutely nothing!

LATISHA: Mr. Chan, you rock. Come here, honey!

MR. CHAN: This bee is bringing the honey, baby! Bzzzzzz . . .

(Latisha and Mr. Chan begin kissing.)

TINA: She's always like this.

TOM: Yeah, Mr. Chan has a tendency towards the ladies.

(Suddenly, Jean-Claude and Sven lunge at one another. They, too, begin kissing.)

TINA: It . . . it must be the heat.

TOM: Uh, yeah . . . yeah . . . the . . . the heat. (Beat.) So . . . so, what brings you here to Doctor DeMarco's?

TINA: Um. The . . . Uh . . . Honestly? Latisha and Jean-Claude. What about you?

TOM: Me too. Mr. Chan and Sven.

(Beat as Tina and Tom watch the puppets necking.)

TINA: Love 'em, but . . . (Beat.) Your . . . your father wasn't a magician with the Tibetan army, was he?

TOM: No. And you don't have a crazy, one-legged aunt?

TINA: No.

TOM: And your parents probably weren't eaten by bunnies during a solar eclipse? (Beat.) You know, I just want to be normal. I want to be able to get a coffee and not worry if Sven is going to complain about holding the scalding cup, let alone his snide comments about the caffeine, the sugar, and the creamer.

(Sven breaks from Jean-Claude.)

SVEN: It's a vasoconstrictor. Don't blame me if you have a massive coronary some lonely night while watching *Desperate Housewives*.

(Sven and Jean-Claude resume kissing.)

TINA: Yes, normal would be nice. Like picking flowers without Jean-Claude calling me *une pansy de la fleur du mal*. Or Latisha complaining about her allergies.

TOM: Hey, pollen is nothing to laugh . . . about. I've . . . I've allergies, too.

TINA: Confession: I bloat up like a balloon if I even see shellfish.

TOM: Mr. Chan too—regular Goodyear blimp.

TINA: Jean-Claude's afraid of heights. You should hear him wail like a baby when I pick apples.

(Jean-Claude breaks from Sven. Mr. Chan and Latisha stop kissing to listen.)

JEAN-CLAUDE: I do not wail—I weep. I weep from the realization that life is fleeting, and your picking an apple is the perfect representation of a life lived and lost. Regardless how perfect the fruit, death shall eat it to the core and, ultimately, cast it aside for the ants and worms to finish. Life is a mime at a convention for the blind.

(Beat. All ponder. Mr. Chan and Latisha, Jean-Claude and Sven lunge back together, kissing more desperately. Beat.)

TOM: It's gotta be the heat.

TINA: Do you think we should try and stop them?

TOM: This is the most time I've had to myself in months. Not . . . not to imply that you're not great company, but . . .

TINA: No, no. I know exactly what you mean. *(Beat.)*

TOM: It's weird, isn't it?

TINA: Incredibly. *(Beat.)* There's got to be a way to get rid of them, don't you think?

TOM: Have you tried doing giant loads of laundry?

TINA: My record is ten in one day—lost two pairs of jeans, three blouses, a sweatshirt, and a skirt I didn't even wash.

TOM: My golden retriever, Mr. Snickers, will chew a lead pipe before them. They blow out the matches, and refuse to go near moving machinery parts. They curl into the fetal position any time I get near scissors, or knives. I've even attempted to talk to a surgeon . . .

TINA: About . . . amputation?

(Beat as Latisha, Mr. Chan, Sven, and Jean-Claude hover threateningly.)

TOM: Yes.

TINA: Uh . . . uh, can you believe how hot it is?

TOM: I've always hated hot weather.

TINA: Me too. The humid, stillness causes the sweat to collect at the nape of your neck and behind your knees.

TOM: And forces your underwear to crawl up your crack . . .

(Latisha and Mr. Chan, Sven and Jean-Claude return to necking.)

TINA: And you can't sleep at night with the windows open . . .

TOM: Because the creepy man in the bushes is going to . . .

TINA: Crawl through the window.

TOM: Exactly.

TOM/TINA: It drives me crazy.

> *(Beat.)*

TOM: Crazy.

TINA: Crazy.

TOM: You're crazy.

TINA: I'm not crazy. You're crazy.

TOM: Nooo.

> *(Beat.)*

TOM/TINA: We're crazy.

> *(Latisha and Mr. Chan separate, postcoital.)*

MR. CHAN: Man without horse doesn't buy saddle.

LATISHA: Yeah, you don't kill the rooster if the hen's happy.

TOM: Well . . . Sven, when he's brooding over the chessboard with a glass of akvavit does claim . . .

> *(Sven disengages from Jean-Claude.)*

SVEN: If time and space are relative, it would seem prudent to assume "reality" is also relative. Therefore, one could postulate each individual has their own inherent reality, thus providing the possibility to surmise those without talking socks on their hands are the minority. And, in regards to genetics, anomalies often . . .

JEAN-CLAUDE: Often fuse opposing poles together, like amore. N'est-ce pas?

TOM: Of course, there's the conundrum . . . what happens to us when they're gone?

TINA: We return to . . . to . . .

JEAN-CLAUDE: Weeping.

SVEN: Brooding.

TOM: You . . . you weep?

TINA: Life is a mime at a convention for the blind. *(Beat.)* And you? You brood?

TOM: Time. Space. Relativity. Sweet, sad, silent . . . consuming . . . oblivion.

TINA: I-crochet. I-disdain-green-M&M's. I-prefer-tea-to-coffee. I-fear . . .

LATISHA: Girl, will you shut up and kiss the One-M fool!

MR. CHAN: Yeah, Tom, thump her with those thin lips.

LATISHA: Kiss him!

> *(Beat.)*

JEAN-CLAUDE: Weep not and . . . slip your hand . . . slowly . . . here.

SVEN: Glide past the dark despair . . . and . . . settle . . . here.

> *(Beat.)*

TINA: But . . . but we could be doomed. Doomed to . . . lonely, ice cream nights of *Desperate Housewives*.

TOM: We . . . we could.

JEAN-CLAUDE: Oui?

TOM: We—you and I. Not oui.

TINA: Right. You and I. Not oui. *(Beat.)*

MR. CHAN: We.

LATISHA: We. *(Beat.)*

TINA: We.

SVEN: Oui.

LATISHA: We.

MR. CHAN: Oui.

SVEN: Wee-wee.

TOM: Oui.

TOM/TINA: We . . .

(Beat.)

TOM: I mean, they seem to have done pretty well. Right?

(Latisha, Mr. Chan, Sven, and Jean-Claude nod in agreement.)

TOM: Why can't we?

TINA: All we . . . us can do is . . . is try.

TOM: Oui?

TINA: Yes. Oui. Us and . . . every . . .

TOM/TINA: One . . . .

(Tina and Tom tentatively kiss. Gradually they continue with enthusiasm. Latisha, Mr. Chan, Jean-Claude, and Sven watch, turn to the audience, take a bow, and resume kissing as the lights fade.)

END OF PLAY

PLAYS FOR
TWO MEN

Downstairs, Upstairs

WENDY MACLEOD

Originally presented by Collaboraction, at the Steppenwolf
Merle Reskin Garage Theatre, Chicago, May 31–July 1, 2007,
as part of the 7th Annual Sketchbook Festival. Directed by
Margot Bordelon. Cast: Mac—J.C. Brown;
Stuart—John Zinn.

CHARACTERS

MAC, thirties, tanned, confident, with an expensive haircut.
STUART, thirties, rumpled, eager, light-deprived.

SETTING

Office with no windows. A lightbulb dangles from the ceiling.

TIME

The present.

• • •

Stuart, in shirtsleeves, sits at a desk in an isolated pool of light. He wears a JC Penney tie askew and taps at a computer terminal. There is the sound of dripping water. Stuart's belongings—a shaving kit, a toothbrush, a pillow—are strewn around. Mac enters, in an expensive suit, finding his way by flashlight.

MAC: There he is! There's my guy! What's the good word? How's life downstairs?

STUART: In the coal mines?

MAC: On the front lines!

STUART: In the trenches?

MAC: Below sea level!

STUART: Not as good as upstairs, I'll bet . . .

MAC: What do you know about upstairs?

STUART: Not enough!

MAC: I bring news of upstairs!

STUART: To the peasants?

MAC: To the plebes!

STUART: To the lowly!

MAC: Are you not men?

STUART: I like to think so.

    How are things? Upstairs?

MAC: You don't want to know.

STUART: I do.

MAC: You'll turn green. You'll vomit with envy.

STUART: Look at me! I'm already green! I'm a seventies appliance! I'm avocado!

MAC: More of a pistachio . . .

STUART: Maybe in full daylight.

MAC: When do *you* see daylight?

STUART: Approximately never.

(The two men laugh.)

STUART: So what brings you down to the netherworld?

MAC: To the slave galley!

STUART: To the bowels of the corporation!

MAC: Funny thing is I don't *think* of it as a corporation.

STUART: No?

MAC: I think of it as a *family.*

(Beat. The two men burst into laughter.)

STUART: Tell me the truth. Do they even know we're down here?

MAC: Do they know . . . Your contributions have been noticed, my friend.

STUART: Bullshit.

MAC: I am a truth-teller.

STUART: Since when?

(They briefly pummel each other.)

MAC: More than noticed. Noted. Your work has been noted.

STUART: As well it should! I've been working my ass off!

MAC: I know you have.

STUART: I sleep here. I *live* here.

MAC: Don't we all?

STUART: No, I mean I actually live here.

(Mac picks up a toothbrush.)

MAC: When was the last time? You went out?

STUART: It must have been that birthday lunch.

MAC: For who? For Martin? When was that?

STUART: Must have been the nineties.

MAC: Was it *that* long ago?

STUART: Well he died in 2000. Remember? It was just after he moved upstairs.

MAC: Your dedication impresses me. But more importantly, it will impress them. They have sent me here. On a fact-finding mission.

STUART: They *sent* you? Is there . . . is there talk of bringing me up?

MAC: There is more than talk. But listen to me carefully, my friend. If they send for you, if your number comes up, say no.

STUART: *Is* my number coming up?

MAC: In exchange for copious amounts of money and unbelievable percs they will demand complete and total fealty. They will demand that you sign a contract. Your 401K will be seized if you so much as return a journalist's phone call!

STUART: How much money are we talking?

MAC: It's not about the money!

STUART: Yeah it is!

MAC: You can be bought, is that what you're saying? You admit you're a prostitute. Now we're just agreeing on the price?

STUART: I would love to be a prostitute! I just haven't had any customers yet! Tell me more about the percs!

MAC: Don't be that guy. Don't fall for the Beemers, the beachfront condos, the box seats at the opera! They're just the cheese in the mousetrap!

STUART: I've never been to the opera.

MAC: You wouldn't like it. The women are fat!

STUART: It sounds like you don't want me upstairs . . .

MAC: Didn't we start out together? Didn't we take turns running to Starbuck's? Don't I know *exactly* how you like your cappuccino?

STUART: Like you remember!

MAC: Venti, skim, dry.

(They embrace.)

MAC: Of course I want you upstairs! Selfishly. I'm just trying to advise you, to apprise you, to *warn* you.

STUART: But they sent you here! To find out about me! Doesn't that demonstrate their good will?

MAC: *(Lowering his voice.)* If they *hadn't* sent me, I couldn't be here. We can only leave to go to the restroom.

STUART: Like kindergarten!

MAC: With guns.

(Pause.)

STUART: Couldn't I just *try* upstairs? I mean, if they make me an offer.

MAC: Upstairs is not a shoe store. "Do these come in black? Do they come in half sizes?" Upstairs is a *commitment*. Once you go upstairs, downstairs is no longer an option. Once you go upstairs, there are no other jobs. The headhunters can no longer *find* you. Once you go upstairs, you can kiss your nostalgic notions of retirement good-bye. There will be no lake house, no grandchildren, no *hobbies*. You will die at your desk and be taken away by janitors. Martin's body was still warm, for Christ sake. His cordovan loafer dangled pathetically from his recently deceased toe. Knowing all that, what will you say when they come to you?

STUART: This company is my home, Mac. I can't imagine working someplace else. I know all the departments, and the heads of all the departments, and when the bagels come, and what the initials stand for, and where my mailbox is and what times of day there's likely to be something in that mailbox. I couldn't leave all that. And if I'm going to work here, if I'm going to stay here, I'd just as soon be upstairs. At least I'd get a window. Wouldn't I?

MAC: You would. You would get a window.

STUART: That's enough for me.

MAC: You *will* get a window. After you sign this.

(*Mac produces a contract.*)

STUART: (*"You shouldn't have."*) Mac.

MAC: We had to be sure.

(*Stuart signs.*)

END OF PLAY

Rats

RON FITZGERALD

Originally commissioned and produced by the stageFARM, at
Cherry Lane Theatre, New York City, October 4–
December 1, 2007, as part of Vengeance, a series of short
plays. Directed by Ari Edelson. Cast: Tom—Michael Mosley;
Ray—David Ross.

CHARACTERS
    TOM
    RAY

SETTING
    Tom's kitchen.

TIME
    The present.

·   ·   ·

Tom sits at the kitchen table watching a TV. He is pointing a gun at a nervous Ray who stands next to the TV changing the channels by hand for Tom.

TOM: Change. Change. Change. Wait. Change. Change. Change. Change. *(Pause.)* Change.

RAY: There's nothing on.

TOM: Change.

RAY: I went through the whole thing.

TOM: Wait. Change.

RAY: Don't you have a *TV Guide* or something?

TOM: Change.

RAY: Or a remote?

TOM: Needs batteries. Change.

RAY: I'm getting tired.

TOM: I have a gun.

RAY: You can't just shoot me.

TOM: You broke into my apartment.

RAY: I didn't break in. I knocked on the door.

TOM: You knocked very loud. Change.

RAY: There's nothing but commercials.

TOM: I like commercials. Change.

RAY: Great, here's a commercial.

TOM: I don't like this one. Change.

RAY: What are you looking for?

TOM: I'm not looking for anything. Change.

RAY: If you tell me what you're looking for, we might find it faster.

TOM: Assuming it exists.

RAY: Change?

TOM: Change.

RAY: You got a radio? We could listen to the radio.

TOM: I shot the radio.

RAY: How come?

TOM: It was a lying little whore.

RAY: I like the radio.

TOM: Well, I killed it. Change.

RAY: Are you going to shoot the television?

TOM: If I do, you'll be the first to know. Do you think I need an Ab Roller?

RAY: Ab Roller?

TOM: Ab Roller. Makes you happy, young, and thin.

RAY: It does?

TOM: Of course. So do cigarettes. Change it.

RAY: Pudding. I guess that makes you happy, young, and thin too.

TOM: Just about everything does. Change.

RAY: Can I show you something?

TOM: It better not be an old, sad, fat person.

RAY: It's a letter.

TOM: Change.

RAY: I'm looking for the person who wrote this letter.

TOM: Change. What letter?

RAY: Save the Children.

TOM: Save the Children. Wait. Change.

RAY: The lady at the advertising agency said you wrote it.

TOM: I don't know anything about any agency.

RAY: You used to work there.

TOM: Define "work."

RAY: She gave me this address. Told me to go see Thomas Murphy.

TOM: Never heard of him.

RAY: It says Thomas Murphy on your mailbox.

TOM: Readily documented. But unwelcome, and, therefore, a nonfact in my book.

RAY: Did you write this letter?

TOM: Look, it's impossible to present unfamiliar thoughts or surprising conclusions in the three-minute stretch between commercials. I'd prefer you stick to the pudding.

RAY: I just want to know if you wrote it.

TOM: Asked and answered. Change.

RAY: I need to know what it means.

TOM: Why?

RAY: I don't understand what it says here.

TOM: It says: send us your money.

RAY: I mean the other parts.

TOM: There are no other parts. Change. Change.

RAY: Wait, I don't—

TOM: You're not changing.

RAY: I don't—

TOM: Change.

RAY: I don't understand.

TOM: Change the fucking channel.

RAY: No. Not until you tell me what it means.

TOM: It doesn't mean anything. It's just a commercial.

RAY: Not that. This.

TOM: That. This. You. Me. There's no difference. There's no control. You spend your life thinking you have control. That you have willpower. Or choice. You can make a choice. But behind that curtain is something else. Or someone else. And you don't get to choose anymore. You don't even recognize where you've got to. There's no patterns. No signs. You break the pattern of how you live. You break the pattern of how *to live*. And then there's nothing to follow. Nothing to be certain of. Nothing to take stock in. There's just . . . you . . . floating away.

(Pause. Then the TV suddenly goes to snow and white noise. Tom stares in shock and awe. Then he screams.)

TOM: AHHHHHHHHHHHHH!

RAY: I didn't do it!

TOM: FIX IT! FIX IT!

(Ray frantically punches buttons. Tom yowls like a kettle that's about to blow. Suddenly the TV screen goes black. There is a moment of stunned silence and then:)

TOM: OH MY GOD, YOU KILLED IT!

RAY: I didn't kill it!

TOM: YOU SON OF A BITCH!

RAY: Maybe it's just resting.

TOM: I NEED MY HAPPY PILLS!

RAY: I can see this is a bad time. How about if I come back later?

TOM: I NEED MY MOTHERFUCKING HAPPY PILLS!

RAY: OK, OK. I—

(Ray frantically searches through the debris.)

TOM: DID YOU FIND THEM YET?

RAY: I'm looking!

TOM: THIS IS DEPRESSING. I WANT TO WATCH TV.

RAY: *(Holds up a Ziploc baggie of colored pills.)* Found them!

TOM: THOSE ARE MY CALM PILLS. I TOOK MY CALM PILLS AL-READY. SEE HOW FUCKING CALM I AM? I COULD LAPSE INTO A COMA, I'M SO CALM AND RELAXED. *(To the TV, prompting, hopeful.)* "My bologna has a first name . . . " *(No luck.)* IF I DON"T GET MY COCKSUCKING PILLS SOMEONE'S GOING TO GET SHOT.

> *(Ray scrambles around the floor, furiously digging through empty take-out cartons and other assorted crap.)*

TOM: I need my happy pills. I get a little squirrelly without my happy pills. Squirrels are clumsy. They make mistakes. You make mistakes, you get fired. You get fired, you lose your health insurance. You lose your health insurance . . . well, let's just say the quality of available brain pharmaceuticals dips considerably. I had to get this shit from the Pizza Guy. "HEY KOOL-AID!"

> *(He looks at the wall, as though Kool-Aid might burst through right on cue. He sags, disappointed.)*

RAY: Do they look like Tic Tacs?

TOM: The Tic Tacs are for my allergies. The happy shit looks like Good & Plenty. "Whazzup? Whazzup? Yo. Where Dookie at? Dookie!"

RAY: Found them.

TOM: Oh thank God.

RAY: They were in your shoe.

TOM: Oh thank Payless. *(Tom grabs the bag of pills and crams all of them into his mouth. His cheeks bulge.)* I need some water.

> *(Ray opens a cabinet to get a glass. He quickly slams it and jumps back.)*

RAY: Gimme the gun.

TOM: The gun? For what?

RAY: I have to get the water.

TOM: The water's quite tame. I assure you.

RAY: There's a rat.

TOM: You found my rat?

RAY: In the cabinet.

TOM: The hell you say.

RAY: I was thinking I could shoot him.

TOM: You can't just go around shooting things, Scooby. That's insane.

RAY: Ray.

TOM: What?

RAY: My name is Ray.

TOM: Tell you what: You watch the TV and I'll make a run for the water.
(Ray sits in Tom's chair and stares at the dark screen. Tom creeps toward the cabinet with the gun. He quietly searches for the rat.)

RAY: Tom?

TOM: What?

RAY: Why did you get fired?

TOM: No reason. *(He fires a shot. BLAM!)* Dammit! He's pretty quick for a big guy.

RAY: That lady at the agency says you got fired 'cause you're all screwed up. Are you all screwed up?

TOM: Here ratty, ratty.

RAY: Cause see . . . if you're all screwed up, maybe Save the Children is all screwed up too.

TOM: Maybe it is.

RAY: I need to know.

TOM: Why?

RAY: My Dad got this in the mail just before they took our house. Save the Children. It says here that: "Poverty undermines the physical, social, intellectual, and emotional development of children." I want to know if that's true. Is that true?

TOM: How should I know?

RAY: The office lady said you wrote it. Save the Children. You wrote: "A root cause is the lack of adequate economic opportunities which enable parents to provide for their children." A root cause of what? You're talking about my life . . . what happened to my family . . . you're talking about me.

TOM: I don't even know you.

RAY: You sent me this letter.

TOM: There's millions of letters out there.

RAY: This one says: "Young people often leave school to seek out income-generating activities to support themselves and their poor families." That's what I did.

TOM: Good for you. Shows initiative.

RAY: "Yet they have few opportunities to gain relevant knowledge and skills."

TOM: Nature can be cruel.

RAY: But it doesn't tell you what to do about it. What are you supposed to do about it?

TOM: I went to college. *(Tom fires: BLAM!)* Crap. I shot the fucking toaster. I think I'm going to need some poison.

RAY: Or better aim.

TOM: Those were warning shots. I can't paint the rat if I blow his head off.

RAY: Why are you going to paint the rat?

TOM: I can't walk in the agency with an unpainted rat. That's completely unprofessional.

RAY: I have no idea what you're talking about.

TOM: OK. Follow the bouncing rat. I was watching *Animal Planet* this morning and I noticed that there are all these *animals* just . . . running around out there.

RAY: That's what animals do.

TOM: Well these animals kinda got stuck in my brain. I even made a note. See?

RAY: This says "Paris Hilton must die."

TOM: The other side.

RAY: "Orangutans do not work for a living."

TOM: Exactly.

(Ray looks at the note.)

RAY: I'm not sure I know what to say.

TOM: Shitbag orangutans just hang out in the rain forest their whole lives. Occasionally they will masturbate, climb a tree, or fling some poo—but I don't think that qualifies as work, do you?

RAY: I don't know.

TOM: Of course it fucking doesn't. Orangutans, baby seals, bald eagles, sea turtles—all that protected shit is getting a free ride. For free. Which is just plain un-American.

RAY: There are no orangutans in America.

TOM: You're missing the point.

RAY: You think animals should pay rent?

TOM: Of course not. What I'm proposing is corporate sponsorship.

RAY: What's that?

TOM: It's like a commercial. I wish I had that rat. The painted rat is going to be my visual aid.

RAY: So the rat's going to get paid?

TOM: No. That's the best part. I get paid. The rat gets fucked.

RAY: I don't get it.

TOM: It's the invisible hand of the free market, turnip seed. You got unemployed animals running around. You got cable channels showing these unemployed animals running around. I'm saying, you take the orangutan, you slap a blue swoosh on his back, and you sell his ass to Nike. *Now, he's fucking working!* He's a contributing member of society. Now every time someone sees him flogging his giant monkey cock, they're thinking: I need new shoes.

RAY: I think you should eat more pills.

TOM: Well it doesn't have to be just orangutans. I mean, tigers got stripes— that could be Adidas. Bears, eagles, seals, turtles—Turtle Wax, come on. It could be anything. You just got to catch it, paint it, and send it off to work.

RAY: You can't do that.

TOM: Not by myself.

RAY: You can't go around slapping logos on everything.

TOM: Not everything. Just the cute shit.

RAY: Rats aren't cute.

TOM: The rat's getting a makeover. Whole new look. He's going to be huge. Mickey Mouse for the eighteen to thirty-five set. Very hip. Very now. Very modern rat.

RAY: You should just leave the animals alone.

TOM: Where's the profit in that? This is high-concept . . . if I don't do it, someone else will.

RAY: You don't know that.

TOM: Nature abhors a vacuum, kid. That's a scientific fact. Just like . . . kill or be killed. The law of the jungle. You can sing *Hakuna Matata* until the cows come home . . . but when the cows get home, you shoot them in the head, you put them on a bun, and you eat them.

RAY: That's different.

TOM: Not to the cow. I know things seem a little . . . upside down right now. This probably isn't what you expected out of life. It certainly isn't what I expected out of life. But that's behind us now. This is the U. S. of A . . . Home of the free and land of the brave. You need to get with the program. You're number one or you're nobody.

RAY: The guy on Fox News says you're either part of the solution or part of the problem.

TOM: That sounds smart.

RAY: So I'm the problem?

TOM: You got any money?

RAY: All I got is this letter.

TOM: Well, there you go.

RAY: So I am the problem. 'Cause I got no money and I got no relevant skills. I'm like the rat.

TOM: Not true. The rat has very relevant skills. He's going to make me rich. Doesn't get more relevant than that.

RAY: No one can get rich off of me.

TOM: Not anymore.

RAY: So they took the house and the land and all the years we put in.

TOM: You strayed from the pack. And so someone had to enforce the morals of our society. Someone had to secure the blessings of liberty for the right-thinking people.

RAY: Which ones are they?

TOM: The ones that hand you the pen and tell you where to sign.

RAY: And they're the solution?

TOM: No, no—pills and television—they're the solution. Be happy, young, and thin forever.

(Tom hands Ray some pills.)

RAY: I can't swallow this.

TOM: Chew on it. Or better yet, chop it up and snort it. The happiness gets to your brain faster.

(Ray chews. Tom resumes his rat hunt.)

RAY: I used to be happy.

TOM: Didn't we all.

RAY: I was happy on the bus here.

TOM: No one is happy on a bus. Eat more pills.

RAY: I had this fantastic dream. I've never had a better dream.

TOM: Was it about me?

RAY: No.

TOM: Oh.

RAY: It starts like this: I'm all alone on my front porch. Just sitting there. Last sounds of summer kinda dying in the twilight. And I'm looking down the road where the sun's just about ducked behind the hills. And I'm waiting. On something. Don't know what. But I know it's good. Something good heading my way. And then this little girl comes along. I don't know how. Or from where. It's just—suddenly, she's there. And she's there with me. And she takes my hand. And I pick her up. And I bounce her on my knee. And she's got this burning red hair. And these cool blue eyes. And she is the most beautiful child I have ever seen. And somehow.

Inside me. At the core. I know. That she is *my* child. And that I am *her* father. And I know . . . that she is bound for unspeakable greatness. I can see it in her smile. I can feel it in her hands. And as we sit on our porch looking out across that great wide world where anything is possible, I know that she is destined to be . . . incredible. And that thought fills me with more joy . . . than I have ever known. In my life.

(Pause. Suddenly Tom leaps toward the sink with a frying pan and a growl. A furious struggle ensues. Tom smashes the rat into submission. After a few more shots just to make sure, he holds up a very large and very dead rat. He smiles proudly to Ray.)

TOM: Full of sound. And furry. And signifying everything in the goddamn world.

RAY: I'm eating the rest of your pills.

(The TV flickers back on, bathing the room in its soothing glow. Tom and Ray turn and stare in mute appreciation. Pause.)

RAY: You want me to change it.

TOM: No. No. This is one of mine.

(Lights fade.)

END OF PLAY

The Train Ride

DANIEL TALBOTT

Originally produced in Melbourne, Australia, as part of the St. Martins Youth Season of New International Work, December 11–14, 2002. Directed by Peter Evans.
Cast: Brother 1—Chris Jefferson; Brother 2—Ben Gerrard.
Also produced by Rising Phoenix Rep at Manhattan Theatre Source, New York City, 2003, as part of their
Flop Night Series. Directed by Brian Roff.
Cast: Brother 1—Denis Butkus; Brother 2—Patch Darragh

CHARACTERS

    BROTHER 1, fifteen years old.

    BROTHER 2, seventeen years old.

SETTING

    A train late at night.

TIME

    The present: dead of winter.

. . .

Sounds of a train and a restless, frightened baby in the background. A back-
pack, digging through it, and a Discman being opened and the sound of but-
tons being pushed. PJ Harvey explodes into the darkness. Lights up on a train
late at night. Two young men sit next to each other. Brother 1 sits quietly
staring out the window at the snow. Brother 2 sits cross-legged, staring ahead,
listening to a Discman. Silence. Brother 2 farts and continues staring ahead,
seemingly unfazed. Brother 1 gets a whiff.

BROTHER 1: Jesus fucking Christ! *(He shifts tighter into the window, shielding*
    his nose with the corner of his jacket.) Disgusting.
    (Brother 2 lets a smile surface on his lips. He continues staring straight ahead
    in silence listening to PJ Harvey.)
    (Silence.)
BROTHER 2: Have you ever wanted to just stand up in public . . . whip your
    dick out and start pissing on people's heads?
BROTHER 1: No.
BROTHER 2: Or like walk into Barnes & Noble on sixty-sixth and take a long
    noisy shit right in the middle of their floor?
BROTHER 1: No.
    (Brother 1 stares out the window trying to ignore Brother 2. Brother 2 stares
    ahead in silence, listening to his Discman.)
BROTHER 2: There was this girl in the park the other day. She was over by one
    of those green benches by the stone amphitheater. You know the ones
    where all the Chinese massagers hang out, selling incense and sex oil,
    stuff? She was sitting cross-legged on this plastic office mat, and she was
    painting a smiley face on this humongous, veiny dildo.
    (No response.)

BROTHER 2: She'd glued like gold loopy earrings on it and hair. And had a little diamond necklace where the shaft hit the balls. It was weird. She was so beautiful. She didn't have a thumb. Just a stub with two butterfly wings tattooed on it and a purple bob wig covered in glitter. She was like some circus freak from when we were young. Big clown wigs and popcorn. Glow sticks.

BROTHER 1: *(Staring out the window at the passing darkness.)* Yeah.

(Silence.)

BROTHER 2: How many times a week do you whack off?

BROTHER 1: Three or four.

BROTHER 2: That's it?!

BROTHER 1: Yeah. Sometimes more. I don't know. Sometimes I don't for weeks. It depends what mood I'm in. Why?

(Brother 2 doesn't respond.)

BROTHER 2: You hear that baby?

BROTHER 1: Yeah.

BROTHER 2: What do you think its mother would do if I walked back there, grabbed it, and started running down the aisle into the dining car?

(Brother 1 looks at Brother 2.)

BROTHER 2: Or if I went back there and just started kicking it in the side of the head a few times? "Shut up, baby! Shut up I says."

(Brother 1 laughs.)

(Silence.)

BROTHER 1: What time do you think we'll get there?

BROTHER 2: Probably around three or four.

BROTHER 1: Do you think Robert will pick us up?

BROTHER 2: I don't know. Maybe. I fucking hate Robert.

(Short pause.)

BROTHER 1: What time do you think it is now?

BROTHER 2: Like one something.

(Silence.)

(Brother 2 takes off his earphones and pushes stop on the Discman. He stands up and stretches using the ceiling of the train. He exits back up the aisle of the train. All lights go down as a single blue-white light comes up on Brother 1. He addresses the audience.)

BROTHER 1: I used to want to be a marine biologist that specialized in killer whales. *Orcinus orca* is their scientific name. The "Lions of the Sea." Perfection in nature. Have you ever seen one of those videos, like *National Geographic*, of an Orca attacking a seal on the beach? It's like the seal's a mortal and some god has called upon a magical sea creature to exact his revenge. It's frolicking on the edge of the shore, barking and rubbing itself on the rocks. And then out of the ocean you see this black and white silhouette materialize and tear through the crest of the wave. Sliding onto the shore, pouncing on the seal with one great thrust, and sucking it back out to sea.

When I was little, my father would read me these books called *Harry the Wayward Whale*. All of them were about this young, rebellious killer whale named Harry that was constantly separating from his pod and going off on secret adventures by himself. Getting into lots of trouble. Pissing off great white sharks, getting caught in fishing nets, stuff like that. And then at the end of all the books, just in the nick of time, his dad would show up and bail him out. There'd be a moral, and then they'd swim off into the sunset together in search of their pod. My dad and I'd always read it out loud together, like a chorus. He'd kiss my head, turn off my desk light, and then I'd fall asleep.

(The light bleeds out on Brother 1. He resumes staring at the passing snow. Brother 2 returns down the aisle of the train and flings himself back into his seat.)

BROTHER 2: Are you sure Robert'll pick us up?

BROTHER 1: I don't know.

BROTHER 2: Did you call him?

BROTHER 1: No.

(Silence.)

BROTHER 2: He's always touching my fucking leg.

BROTHER 1: He does not.

BROTHER 2: He does too. And whenever I'm taking a piss at Dad's house he always finds a reason to walk in and sneak a peak at my dick.

BROTHER 1: That's completely not true. He's always been cool to both of us and you know it.

BROTHER 2: Do you know what Robert did before he met Dad? He was a fucking prostitute. He used to suck guys' dicks for money. He's even in a porno.

(Brother 1 is silent.)

BROTHER 2: How do you think I found out Dad was a fag?

BROTHER 1: What were you doing watching a gay porn movie?

BROTHER 2: Ha, ha, ha. Funny! Fuck you. *(Short silence.)* I feel like I can't breathe on this fucking train. I feel like I'm going to throw up. I keep saying stupid shit. *(Beat.)* What time is it?

BROTHER 1: I don't know. I think we're still in Connecticut though.

(Brother 2 lies back in his seat and reclines the chair.)

BROTHER 1: Do you remember that time Dad took us whale watching and you got really sick?

BROTHER 2: No.

BROTHER 1: We were both really little. I think you were like seven or eight and I was like five or something? Mom packed us lunch boxes with peanut butter and jelly sandwiches and Nutter Butters. And you stole my sandwich and ate it and told me that a bird had swooped down and picked it off while I wasn't looking. And that if I wanted it back I had to go and steal one of the bird's babies and hold it for ransom until it gave in and returned the sandwich. *(Beat.)* That was the first time I saw Robert. I mean the first time I was introduced to him was five years ago, but he was talking to Dad that day on the boat.

BROTHER 2: I don't remember that.

BROTHER 1: I do. *(Short silence.)* Did Dad ever touch you?

BROTHER 2: No. *(Pause.)* You?

BROTHER 1: No. But he would uh . . . in the bath sometimes, he'd have me touch him.

(Silence.)

BROTHER 2: Last night I had a dream all this was going to happen. I dreamed about the phone call. About Aunt Martha picking us up . . . About the train. *(Short pause.)* There was this room. I could hear water dripping and footsteps and for some reason, my dick was out and there was blood all over the head of it and all over my feet. Dad was in the middle of the room and his skin was white like porcelain and it stretched out into every corner. Into the walls, till it became the walls and each time he breathed, the room would breathe with him. At first it seemed easy. He seemed proud. Proud the breath was steady and his own. It was quiet except for the air passing through his nostrils, rhythmically. I smiled and he opened his mouth to smile back and water exploded out of him like vomit. I could feel it hit my face and I thought I was going to throw up. Then his eyes went black and he just split . . . like a balloon, spilling over my feet, washing the blood clean.

(Silence.)

BROTHER 1: Do you think Robert'll be there?

BROTHER 2: I don't know. If he's not, we can always call a taxi and go to the hospital by ourselves.

(Silence.)

(Brother 2 puts his earphones back on. Gets his jacket from underneath his seat, pushes play, then lies back in the chair, pulling the jacket over his head. Short silence. All lights go down and a single blaring blue-white light comes up on Brother 1. He addresses the audience.)

BROTHER 1: Killer whales are often confused for whales when in fact they're dolphins. They're the largest dolphin known to man and have been living in the ocean for centuries. Many scientists believe they're the most intelligent creatures on earth. I believe they're the closest creatures to God. When you watch them swimming in the wild, with their young, you know you're witnessing genius. Perfection in nature. I remember June 17, 1997, better than any day of my life. I remember a Chinese food restaurant in Mill Valley, California, where I lived with my brother and mother and father. I remember my father ordering chicken fried rice 'cause he knew it was my favorite. I remember: Love. Family. Man. Robert. I remember some cheesy Bette Midler song. I remember: Love. Sorry. And Sick. I remember the car . . . a new car . . . a Mercedes. And rain. And the feel of my face against the black leather of the back seat. There was silence and the sound of windshield wipers. I dreamt I was on a boat in the middle of the ocean and the sound of the rain faded into the sounds of the sea. I was watching . . . waiting for a glimpse of God. And beside me was my dad, with his fishing pole and favorite black and red checkered flannel shirt. We were both drinking cocoa, watching the horizon. And I was happy.

END OF PLAY

Two from the Line

MICHAEL LOUIS WELLS

Originally produced at Ensemble Studio Theatre/Lexington
Center for the Arts, New York City, July 26, 2007.
Directed by Rebecca Schlossberg. Cast: Al—Andy Bergh;
Ed—Michael Rosete.

ED, late twenties.
AL, late twenties.

SETTING
A starkly barren one-room apartment in an old tenement-style building in New York's Hell's Kitchen neighborhood.

TIME
The present.

. . .

In black, we hear Marv Albert calling a New York Knicks game. At rise: We discover Ed and Al drinking beer in the blue glow of the small television in Al's apartment—a bare, cheap room in Hell's Kitchen.

AL: Yes! Yes! Yes!

ED: I feel worthless.

AL: Huh?

ED: I'm broke. I'm losin' my hair. My girlfriend dumped me. I'm a failure. Worthless.

AL: You're not losin' your hair.

ED: I am! I am, it's thinning all over the place.

AL: Looks fine to me.

ED: I had a dream about sucking your dick.

AL: What?!

ED: The summer we graduated. The Summer of Cheap Beer. I never told you. When my gramma died. My greatgramma. I was sittin' there in the funeral home. They're playin' the organ music and everything. Good old Phoebe's lyin' up there in a box. And I'm thinking about how I'd maybe like to suck your cock.

AL: So . . . what? You're gay? Are you telling me that you're gay?

ED: Six?

AL: Huh?

ED: Eighty-nine, eighty-five. No. They're down four.

AL: Hold up.

ED: When is Isiah gonna bring this fuckin' team around?

AL: Forget the game for a minute. What are you telling me?

ED: That's a shooting foul?!

AL: Uh . . . yeah. I think so.

ED: They're in the penalty?!

AL: Now.

ED: *(Beat.)* I was sittin' there in my three-piece powder-blue polyester leisure suit, sweating, and thinking about the day I first got high with you and Robertson down the island park. We kept doing hits off his waterpipe, but I didn't feel anything, so we started holding our breath and running down that big hill by the ball field, trying to hyperventilate. We drove the truck over to Farmer Jack's and ate a blueberry pie outta the box with our fingers. It was the summer we worked for the city. It was hotter than shit. And we cooled off drinkin' Wyler's lemonade outta a ball jar in your parents' basement sittin' around in our underwear listening to *Jungle Book* for grins. *(Beat.)* I'm just thinking all this while the service is goin' on and wonderin' what it would be like to suck your dick. And it made me feel good. Until I remember that like my mom is sitting there. And Milt's dad. And Reverend Wesley. And I'll probably fry in hell for thinking about giving out blow jobs while my gramma's being laid out.

AL: So, uh . . . Howd'ya feel, now?

ED: Worthless. Like I'm never gonna grow up. Never gonna fall in love. Never. Worthless.

AL: No, I mean . . . Do you still feel like suckin' me off?

ED: Not particularly. *(Beat.)* No. Definitely not.

AL: Oh.

ED: So, don't worry.

AL: I'm not. I mean, I wasn't. Worried.

ED: Good. *(Beat.)* Got any food on ya?

AL: Sure. Whaddya need?

ED: Sandwich?

AL: Bread's on top of the fridge. Cheese's in the crisper.

ED: The what?

AL: Vegetable drawer.

ED: Whaddid you call it?

AL: The crisper.

ED: *(Beat.)* OK. *(He exits.)*

AL: Shit!

ED: *(Re-entering.)* What?

AL: That's five on Marbury.

ED: Fuck me.

(They stare at the screen. In a moment, Ed drifts back into the kitchen. Al calls off to him.)

AL: You seein' that new babe?

ED: *(Off.)* Lisel?

AL: You seein' her?

ED: *(Off.)* We caught a movie uptown the other night.

AL: And . . . ?

ED: And we sat around her place on the floor till three, smoking cigs and discussing our former sordid sex lives.

AL: Yeah?

ED: And she told me how she still loves her ex and that he's still her best friend and all but that he's not The One. And . . .

AL: Uh-huh.

ED: And how hard it was for her to break it off since they were practically engaged and that they didn't speak for months and then he called up all angry and everything and she took him to lunch and fucked him one last time in the car and he started crying so she's decided she's not gonna see him anymore—even tho' he is like her best friend because he'll just try to talk her into staying in the relationship and she just has to go with what she feels because that's her only rule and so many people settle for second best and would I give her a spanking before we do it. *(Re-entering with sandwich, Ed comes to stop, staring at the screen.)* What was that?

AL: Steps.

ED: Shit.

AL: So, did you . . .?

ED: *(Beat.)* Oh. No. She was tired. I went home.

AL: You gonna see her again?

ED: I was.

AL: What happened?

ED: Last night she stood me up.

AL: Huh.

ED: You feel like renting *Dead Ringers* again?

AL: MAYbee.

(They watch.)

ED: How's this guy from the line?

AL: Surprisingly average. *(Counting.)* Five, six, seven. He always dribbles seven times before he—

ED: Clang!

AL: Did I say?

ED: Here we go.

AL: Dee-fense!

ED: I think I gave Ramon a scare.

AL: That salsa guy that lives next to ya?

ED: Pick him up! Yeah, I was . . .

AL: Uh-huh.

ED: . . . sitting in Maria's old closet screaming "fuck you" at the top of my lungs and hitting myself over the head with my American College Dictionary . . .
Goal tending?!

AL: Yup.

ED: He never broke the cylinder!

AL: What can I tell ya?

ED: Christ! *(Beat.)* Anyway, the doorbell rings but I keep on with the primal scream therapy and self-rolfing bit. Finally, about five minutes later I hear him outside my window, real softlike "Ed? Ed?"

AL: Ramon?

ED: So—yeah—I get up and stick my head out the window. And he's stickin' his head out the window. And he's like, "Are j'ou OK? My wife was worried." And I'm like, "yeah, yeah. I was on the phone."
(Ed finds this quite humorous and begins cackling somewhat insanely. Al regards him warily.)

AL: You got some kinda health plan at work?

ED: Medical, dental, vision—the lot. That is one thing I will say for them.

AL: Uh-huh.

ED: The ass-sprays. Why?

AL: I dunno. Just . . . Well, you know where you're at, right?

ED: Where I'm at?

AL: You probably do. But, all I'm sayin' is maybe . . . Maybe you oughta think about seein' somebody.

ED: What, like a shrink, you mean?

AL: It could maybe help.

ED: Help what?

AL: Help you get all this stuff you're talking, ya know—out. About Maria or . . .

ED: Baseline!

AL: Or like, um, anything that might be botherin' ya.
(Ed stares at him blankly, beat.)

AL: It might help. It helped a friend of mine.

ED: Who?

AL: What?

ED: Who did it help?

AL: It helped my friend Hilary.

ED: You have a friend named Hilary?

AL: Yeah.

ED: Guy or a girl?

AL: A girl. I mean, it's a girl's name.

ED: Not necessarily. There have been some very famous men named Hillary.

AL: Like who?

ED: British explorers and whatnot. Sir Hillary of such and so.

AL: Right. Well, this Hilary of mine was a girl. And she had this tough breakup with this guy, and she, well, she kinda went nuts.

ED: Nuts?

AL: I'm not sayin' you are.

ED: Nuts?

AL: She kinda did. Followin' the guy all over the place. Turnin' up at his work. Calling him over and over and just hanging up.

ED: How did you know it was her?

AL: I just did.

ED: Gotcha!

AL: What? *(Beat.)* Oh.

ED: Gotcha.

AL: OK, so I was the guy. And, I guess . . . I dunno. I was pretty shitty to her.

ED: Whaddid ya do?

AL: Huh?

ED: Whaddid you do that was so shitty?

AL: I dunno. I just was. The point is . . .

ED: The point is you wanna help me, right?

AL: Yes! Yes, and . . .

ED: So, tell me what you did.

AL: I don't know! I don't remember! *(Al exits to the kitchen, then quickly re-enters.)* OK. Here's one thing I did.

ED: Good.

AL: This really sucked.

ED: Great.

AL: She bought me these flowers once. She came home after work one day with these flowers in a little vase and gave it to me. No reason. "Just because you're my Snail Man," she said.

ED: "My Snail Man"?

AL: *(Beat, guardedly.)* Yeah.

ED: *(Beat, with awe and longing.)* That. Is. Cool.

AL: Anyway, the whole time, like during that entire time that we were livin' together . . .

ED: Wait a minute.

AL: Now, what?

ED: You were living with her?

AL: Did I just say?

ED: Where was I?

AL: Two summers ago.

ED: What?

AL: Think about it.

ED: Two summers . . . ? *(Beat.)* Oh.

AL: OK?

ED: Yeah. Yikes.

AL: Got your bearings, now?

ED: I'll never live that down, will I?

AL: Doubtful. Anyway . . .

ED: Ugh.

AL: So the whole time I was seeing and living with Hilary, I was in love with another woman. The entire time. And she was married.

ED: She was . . . ?!

AL: I'm not goin' into that—

ED: What?!

AL: —just now. I'm not. But the whole time I was in love with someone else. It wasn't exactly fair because I knew how much Hilary was into it, ya know, into me, I kinda let her—nice hands! I let her hang around. I kinda got off on it, I guess.

ED: Who wouldn't?

AL: Right?

ED: But you didn't love her.

AL: No. But I did like her. I liked her a lot. But . . .

ED: It's not the same.

AL: Who's tellin' this?

ED: It's not the same at all.

AL: I think I started to resent it. Like how much she liked me. But instead of saying anything I just started to fill this vase, the one she brought me that time, I started filling it with cigarette butts. Dirty disgusting cigarette butts. And there it was, ya know? Right where she could see it, have to look at it every day. And one day . . . one day she asked for it back. Things were kind of deteriorating anyway. We weren't really even sleeping together anymore. She just . . .

ED: Uh-huh.

AL: She just walked up to me very calmly and in a quiet quiet voice asked for it back. Ya know? And all I could do was just go, OK. I tried to say it real cool, but, I dunno. I was ashamed.

ED: And then what happened?

AL: Well, that was it, ya know? She packed her stuff and left.

ED: She moved out?

AL: That day, yeah. And then like I said she went through this whole thing.

ED: Callin' you up and stuff.

AL: Yeah. But she started seein' this guy twice a week . . .

ED: The shrink guy.

AL: Exactly. And it really really helped her she said. I know it did. I ran into her once after and she was cool. And then she moved to London.

ED: Makes sense.

AL: *(Nodding.)* Right? *(Beat.)* What?

ED: That's where they belong.

AL: Who?

ED: People named Hillary.

AL: Oh.

ED: They belong in Merry Olde England.

AL: I guess.

ED: Except for the one. You know who I mean.

AL: Right.

ED: She's good. But all the rest of them. The extra ones, I'm sayin' . . .

AL: Sure.

ED: Ouch!

AL: What?

ED: Bit myself. *(They return their attention to the game.)*

AL: What the hell is that?!

ED: Ow.

(Ed gingerly touches his cheek. Al jumps to his feet excited by the action on the screen.)

AL: Whoa whoa whoa!!!

(A tremendous amount of blood begins seeping from Ed's mouth.)

ED: I'm bleedin'.

AL: Get back! Get back!

ED: How the fuck did I do that?

AL: That was three, right?!

ED: Shit.

AL: What?

ED: It's nothing.

AL: You're bleeding.

ED: I know.

AL: Whaddid ya do?

ED: Bit myself.

AL: Huh?

ED: Bit myself in the mouth.

AL: Shit.

ED: Yeah.

AL: Whaddya want? Some ice or something?

ED: Ice?

AL: To slow the bleeding, yeah.

ED: Ice?

AL: No?

ED: I'm bleedin'!

AL: I know! Do ya want . . . ? Whaddya want?

ED: I want you to hold me.

AL: What?!

ED: To stop the bleeding. I want you to hold me and make it all better.

AL: I'll get some ice. *(Al moves toward the kitchen.)*

ED: Al!

AL: I'll get that ice.

ED: Don't move!

AL: What?

 (Ed grabs Al around the waist.)

AL: Get the fuck off!

ED: Hold me! Hold me!

AL: Fuckin' . . . Get the fuck offa me!

 (Ed and Al struggle on the floor. Ed winds up on top.)

AL: Fuck! Get off!

ED: Hold me! Hold me!

AL: Shit!

ED: Tell me I'm the only one!

AL: What the fuck is wrong with you?

ED: I want you to hold me. Give me a hug.

AL: Not like this!

ED: What?

AL: Get offa me!

ED: Not until you give me a hug.

(Beat. Al gives Ed a brief hug.)

ED: Good. Now, tell me that you love me.

AL: No way, man.

ED: You don't love me?

AL: Get off!

ED: Tell me!

AL: Christ! You're bleeding all over . . .

ED: I love you, Al.

AL: This is deeply wrong.

ED: You're my best friend! Are you saying . . . ? Why don't you love me?

AL: Got a minute?

ED: What? Is it the gay thing?

AL: Get off!

ED: Because I'm not. A buttbird. A rear admiral. I don't wanna bugger you. I don't wanna suck you off.

AL: You just told me you did!

ED: I was grieving! Fuck! That was some cosmic subconscious stuff I didn't understand. I wanna hold you. Like wrestling.

AL: *(Beat.)* What?

ED: I don't wanna fuck you! I wanna fuck girls. Women. Girls. And as soon as I do, as soon as I fall for some girl/woman/girl, my guts get ripped open, she spews her putrid rotting maggot load inside me and my guts start sizzling. This is your brain. This is your brain on chicks. Any questions?! I start spilling stuff after we've fucked, after the fall, *(Singing demonically like Johnny Rotten doing Engelbert Humperdinck.)* "af-ter the lov-in!," that I wouldn't, shouldn't, tell anyone ever!

That whole private library of fear and prejudice and all the stuff I don't even wanna think about gets laid bare. She just like peruses it and then cuts out. She flees the scene of the crime, and I'm left here like I've not only been raped, my soul has been burgled! Fuuuuuuuuck!!!

AL: So, whaddya want me to do?

ED: Say you'll be there for me.

AL: Whaddya mean?

ED: Just tell me you're not gonna pull one of those bank jobs on my soul.

AL: You're so fuckin' dramatic, Ed.

ED: Tell me!!!

AL: All right. You can count on me.

ED: Really?

AL: Absolutely.

ED: *(Sighing hugely.)* Fuck. *(Beat.)* Thanks, man.

AL: It's all right. *(Beat.)* Ed?

ED: Yeah?

AL: Ya wanna get off me, now?

ED: Oh, sure, pal.

> *(Ed lets Al up. Al immediately pins Ed to the ground.)*

AL: Don't you ever do that to me, again!

ED: I won't.

AL: I mean, never!

ED: I won't. I'm sorry.

AL: *(Beat.)* All right, then. Apology accepted.

> *(Al lets Ed up. They stand staring at each other for some time.)*

AL: Beer?

ED: Sure.

> *(Al exits to the kitchen.)*

AL: *(Off.)* Who won?

ED: What?

AL: *(Off.)* The game? Who won?

ED: I dunno. There's a movie on now.

> *(Al enters with two beers.)*

AL: Switch over to TNT. They got the Sixers comin' on at ten.

ED: They're playing on the coast?

AL: Golden State, yeah.

> *(Al hands Ed a beer.)*

ED: Thanks, man.

AL: What're friends for?

> *(They pop their beers and drink together. Music leads lights quickly to black.)*

END OF PLAY

PLAYS FOR
TWO WOMEN

Farewell and Adieu

JACK NEARY

First performed as part of the Boston Theater Marathon, May 20, 2007. Produced by New Century Theatre, Smith College, Northampton, Massachusetts. Directed by Jack Neary. Cast: Clarice—Ellen Colton; Bethel—Bobbie Steinbach.

CHARACTERS
    CLARICE, a woman around sixty.
    BETHEL, a woman around sixty.

SETTING
    A parlor in a funeral home.

TIME
    The present.

•   •   •

We can see two relatively ornate chairs placed in the corner of the room. That's pretty much all we need to see. Clarice sits in one of the chairs. She is dressed smartly in black. She opens her purse and takes out a brochure, which she begins to read as Bethel enters. She is dressed sharply in black.

BETHEL: Oh. You're still here.

CLARICE: I saw you in the receiving line. You think I wouldn't wait?

BETHEL: *(Sits.)* I know how you feel about it, so I thought you'd just scurry . . .

CLARICE: You know how I feel about what?

BETHEL: Death.

CLARICE: *(Accedes.)* I'm not a big fan.

BETHEL: I know.

CLARICE: So . . . how'd she look to you?

BETHEL: Deceased.

CLARICE: Besides that.

BETHEL: There is no besides that. Deceased is deceased. You're dead, you look dead.

CLARICE: I thought she looked fabulous.

BETHEL: For dead, yes. I'll tell you one thing, it was pretty obvious she didn't do her own makeup.

CLARICE: *(Chuckles.)* That's for sure.

BETHEL: Last time she looked that young was when she played that hooker in *Irma La Douce* in 1967.

CLARICE: There's a role she didn't have to research.

BETHEL: Amen. I should look that good when I'm dead.

CLARICE: Leave your head shot with your next of kin. They do a superb job here.

BETHEL: They do.

CLARICE: Janet Plaistek, when she died, they didn't come here. They brought her over to Tremblays, laid her out, opened the box, she scared the shit outa the grandchildren. Tremblay's called here, Marty goes over and squeezes her face into something presentable.

BETHEL: Janet was always very malleable.

CLARICE: She was.

BETHEL: Marty from here went over there?

CLARICE: He did.

BETHEL: I didn't think there would be cooperation in that regard.

CLARICE: Marty had a price. Ever since then, when Tremblay's is overbooked, they refer them to here.

BETHEL: Why is Tremblay's so popular, do you think?

CLARICE: It's right across the street from Appleby's.

BETHEL: Of course. *(Refers to brochure.)* What's that?

CLARICE: Next season. *The Lyric.*

BETHEL: Anything for us?

CLARICE: *(Points to other room.)* There is now.

BETHEL: *(Takes brochure.)* Lemme see. *(Reads; stops.)* Oh. My God.

CLARICE: You see it.

BETHEL: I see it.

CLARICE: Jumped right out at me.

BETHEL: Well, it's about time.

CLARICE: Fraulein Schneider.

BETHEL: We've been trying to get him to do that for . . .

CLARICE: Years.

BETHEL: And there it is . . .

CLARICE: There it is.

BETHEL: Closing the season.

CLARICE: As it should.

BETHEL: Finally.

CLARICE: Finally.

BETHEL: The part of my life.

CLARICE: The part of your . . . *(Catches herself.)* What?

BETHEL: Fraulein Schneider. The part of my life.

CLARICE: Your life?

BETHEL: Who else's life?

CLARICE: Who else's life do you think?

BETHEL: Clarice . . . Clarice . . . no . . . no . . . this part . . . this part . . . is . . . beyond your ken.

CLARICE: Beyond my what?

BETHEL: Your ken. Your capacity. Your ability to connect.

CLARICE: But your ken, it's within reach.

BETHEL: There will be no reaching. When I play the part, Fraulein Schneider and I will be as one.

CLARICE: As one what?

BETHEL: It's an expression.

CLARICE: It usually is, with you.

BETHEL: Don't be jealous.

CLARICE: Jealous of what? You don't have the part yet. We'll have to audition.

BETHEL: Clarice . . . why would you put yourself through that?

CLARICE: Put myself through? I have just as good a chance of getting that part as you do.

BETHEL: Darling . . . Sweetheart . . . Darling . . . it's a musical.

CLARICE: What am I, a jockey? I know it's a musical.

BETHEL: Well . . . I mean . . . to audition . . . you'll have to trot out that . . . song you do.

CLARICE: What's wrong with my song? My audition song never fails to raise eyebrows.

BETHEL: Well, of course it raises eyebrows, Clarice. Not many sixty-year-old actresses audition with "Trouble in River City."

CLARICE: It shows my rhythm.

BETHEL: *(Reaches into her own bag.)* Look . . . there are plenty of other roles you can audition for. Here. *The Reagles. (Points to brochure.)* There. You can audition for that.

CLARICE: *(Looks.)* That? I hate kids. And I can't play the guitar.

BETHEL: Oh, you're too old for that part.

CLARICE: Well, what other part is there?

BETHEL: Mother Superior!

CLARICE: She's onstage for four minutes!

BETHEL: But she has a wonderful song.

CLARICE: Wonderful? When was the last time you forded a stream? No! I got as much a shot at landing Fraulein Schneider as you do. I'm auditioning! And I'm gonna get it!
(They both sit rigidly for a couple of seconds. Then, gently, Bethel begins to sing, as dramatically as possible given the location.)

BETHEL: "How the world can change. It can change like that. Due to one little word . . ."

CLARICE: *(Sings.)* "Amateur."

(Another longish beat, both women staring forward, incensed.)

BETHEL: So . . . it's come to this.

CLARICE: What? What has it come to?

BETHEL: It's come to she's gone. There's only you and me left.

CLARICE: Oh. *(Beat; gets it.)* Oh.

BETHEL: She was our buffer.

CLARICE: It never occurred to me. *(Beat.)* That we were being buffed.

BETHEL: In the past, we'd audition, she'd audition. She'd get the part. We'd bitch about it. *(Beat.)* We'd audition again, she'd audition again, she'd get the part again. We'd bitch about it . . .

CLARICE: Again.

BETHEL: She was our crutch. Our buffer and our crutch.

CLARICE: The Old Crutch and Buffer. *(Beat.)* Sounds like a tavern in Gloucester. *(Chuckles.)*

BETHEL: This is not funny, Clarice. It's over. It's just you against me now.

CLARICE: Are you sure about this?

BETHEL: Think about it. Without her around, who are you gonna bitch about?

CLARICE: Well I can't bitch about you. You're my friend.

BETHEL: Nor can I bitch about you. You're my friend. So the question is . . . *(Beat.)* the question . . . is . . .

CLARICE: What? What is the question?

BETHEL: The question is . . . do we remain friends . . . or do we become each other's bitterest enemy?

CLARICE: That's our only option?

BETHEL: I believe . . . I believe it is. Yes.

CLARICE: Wow.

BETHEL: Indeed. *(Beat.)* Wow.

(A longish moment. The ladies stare into space.)

BETHEL: Unless . . .

CLARICE: Unless? Unless what?

BETHEL: Unless . . . we alternate.

CLARICE: Alternate what?

BETHEL: Auditions. We alternate auditions. When it comes time to vie for a role . . . we don't.

CLARICE: We don't what?

BETHEL: Vie.

CLARICE: We don't vie.

BETHEL: No. An audition comes up, if it's my turn to go, I go. If it's your turn, you go. Now that she's no longer part of the equation, it's highly likely we'll end up cast every time. We don't vie, and we remain friends. I think it's a brilliant idea under the circumstances.

CLARICE: *(Beat.)* You may be on to something.

BETHEL: It's the only solution.

CLARICE: Well thank God.

BETHEL: Yes.

CLARICE: The last thing we want to do is jeopardize our friendship.

BETHEL: Yes.

CLARICE: Over a silly role.

BETHEL: Yes.

CLARICE: A role either of us could play.

BETHEL: Yes.

CLARICE: Like Fraulein Schneider.

BETHEL: Yes. *(Beat.)* What?

CLARICE: I go first.

BETHEL: What?

CLARICE: *(Digging in bag.)* You don't wanna vie, fine. I go first. I audition for Fraulein Schneider. You climb every mountain.

BETHEL: What are you digging?

CLARICE: *(Pulls out cell phone.)* I'm booking the audition. First one to book it gets it. *(Starts to punch in full number.)*

BETHEL: *(Digs in her bag.)* That's not fair! *(Gets cell phone, presses one button.)*

CLARICE: I'M SAVING OUR FRIENDSHIP!

BETHEL: AHA!

CLARICE: WHAT!!!

BETHEL: *(Shows phone.)* Speed dial. *(Into phone.)* Hello, Spiro?

CLARICE: You have him on speed dial!

BETHEL: *(To Clarice.)* I'm a professional! *(Into phone.)* Spiro? Bethel. How are you, sweetheart? . . . Good. Good.

CLARICE: *(Mutters.)* Bitch!

BETHEL: Listen, I'd like to book an audition for *Cabaret. (Beat.)* What? *(Beat.)* You're kidding. *(Beat.)* No. No. That's . . . perfectly understandable.

CLARICE: What's perfectly understandable?

BETHEL: *(Into phone.)* Yes. *(Beat.)* Yes, she was. Yes. Well. Good-bye, then. *(Clicks off; beat.)*

CLARICE: What???

BETHEL: He scrapped the show.

CLARICE: What? Why?

BETHEL: He picked it for her. She dropped dead. He cancelled. *(Beat.)* He's doing *Full Monty.*

(Long staring beat.)

CLARICE: Even from the grave, she buffs.

(Bethel stands abruptly.)

CLARICE: Where are you going?

BETHEL: *(With meaning.)* I didn't sign the book. I thought I'd leave her a note. *(Starts off.)*

CLARICE: *(Jumps up, stops her.)* Better not!

BETHEL: *(As Clarice seats her again.)* You're right.

(Another long staring moment. Then, Clarice sings.)

CLARICE: "How the world can change. It can change like that . . ."

(Another long beat.)

BETHEL: Like that.

(They look at each other, then their heads turn, slowly and simultaneously, toward the other room. They look at each other again, reach out, take each other's hands, smile wistfully, then stare out again as the lights fade to black.)

END OF PLAY

Female Dogs

BARBARA LINDSAY

First produced by Theatre Inspirato at Alchemy Theatre,
Toronto, June 7–16, 2007 as part of Trapped Spaces,
2nd Annual Toronto Ten-Minute Festival.
Directed by Alexandra Riccio. Cast: Kyla—Kelly-Marie
Murtha; Sandy—Manuela Nudo.

CHARACTERS

SANDY, thirties, attractive, happily married and secure in her husband's affections. She is sympathetic to Kyla's sadness—up to a point.

KYLA, Sandy's friend, thirties, attractive, and unhappily single. Disappointments in love have left her bitter, sarcastic, and envious of those lucky women who are coupled and content. She did not used to be mean.

SETTING

A nice restaurant/bar.

TIME

The present: evening, happy hour.

• • •

Lights up. At rise: Sandy and Kyla sit at a table with drinks and snacks.

KYLA: Look at her.

SANDY: Where?

KYLA: Behind you right. Miss Bottle-Bought-Blonde in the red sweater, with the Marlboro Man.

SANDY: What about her?

KYLA: She's ruining him for other women.

SANDY: What are you talking about?

KYLA: Well, look at her. Oh Jesus, Sandy, be subtle. You see what I mean?

SANDY: Well. She is sort of classically pretty.

KYLA: No, you innocent, I'm not talking about that. You're pretty, I'm pretty, lots of women are pretty. Men don't really care about that. I'm talking about that sweater. I've seen it at Bloomies. It did not come with those buttons. And you see that? How she's sewn little glittery bits here and there? Oh for God's sake, don't stare.

SANDY: I'm trying to see. So?

KYLA: So this is a woman who sews new sparkly buttons and sequins on her new red sweater. And you see how it stretches just so across her perfect boobs? Not slutty but very, very suggestive, very much an invitation? "Touch these, oh please, these are just dying to be touched, you know you want to, oh please, oh please."

SANDY: Kyla, what's going on with you today?

KYLA: And I'll bet you fifty dollars her underwear matches. Swear to God. For another ten, I'll even bet I could tell you the color.

SANDY: A, you could never prove it, and B, what is wrong with you?

KYLA: Lavender. Ten bucks on lavender.

SANDY: Does it strike you as disturbing that you're spending this much time thinking about another woman's underwear? Why are you being so—?

KYLA: And listen to that laugh. *(She quietly imitates the laugh.)* All tinkly soprano with the vibrato just so. I'll bet she took classes. When she dumps him, and she will, I'm telling you, he's going to be ruined for any other woman.

SANDY: Oh no. Did you call Danny?

KYLA: Do you know what color my underwear is?

SANDY: Call me crazy, but I never once thought to wonder. Did you call Danny when I told you not to?

KYLA: Blue panties with sagging elastic and an ivory, formerly white, bra.

SANDY: You did, didn't you. You called Danny. Oh Kyla, when are you going to learn? Was it awful?

KYLA: I hate that woman. She's evil. That's how she wins.

SANDY: Will you please stop it? You're being horrible. It's not her you're mad at. Why did you call Danny? You knew what he would say.

KYLA: Ten more bucks says she's a serial boyfriend stealer.

SANDY: I'm serious. I will not have this conversation. You're drowning in bile here, and I absolutely will not join you. You've been howling after Danny for five months now. I know it's painful, but it didn't work out, and it's time to move on. Before everybody can't stand you. It would be different if you were sad, but you've gotten hard and rancorous and mean.

KYLA: Well, women wouldn't be such bitches if men weren't such dogs.

SANDY: Men are not dogs.

KYLA: Yes they are.

SANDY: No they're not. Men are lovely.

KYLA: Oh, puke.

SANDY: OK, maybe not some, but most men are. They are gorgeous, mysterious creatures put on earth to allow us to experience our womanliness.

KYLA: Oh my good lord. Are you completely insane? Have you not been paying attention to the relationship holocaust that's all around you?

SANDY: I like men. I adore them.

KYLA: That's because you've got one.

SANDY: OK, yes. I admi , it doesn't hurt. But still, I know so many really kind, decent—

KYLA: You've forgotten what it's like to be single. Men are dogs, they're pigs, they're shallow, self-absorbed, cheating bastards.

SANDY: What turned you so cynical? I know Danny left you, but it wasn't as though he broke into your apartment and stole your checkbook, or killed your cat, or slept with your mom or anything. He just changed his mind.

KYLA: He didn't just change his mind. He changed his mind, erased me from his memory bank, and got Roberta Picklepuss pregnant two months later.

SANDY: Oh Kyla. Oh honey. I didn't know.

KYLA: Yeah, I just found out a few days ago. From Miss "And-I'm-hardly-vomiting-at-all-tra-la" herself.

SANDY: I'm so sorry.

KYLA: Don't be sorry for me. Be sorry for Roberta, who now has a bastard father for her bastard baby. Fatherhood isn't going to keep that dog faithful.

SANDY: When a man is really committed to you, you don't have to keep him. He keeps himself.

KYLA: You know what? You make me sick. You really do. It's all platitudes with you. You're so far removed from the hell of the meat market, you've convinced yourself that men are these worthy creatures who only need the love of a good woman to turn them into princes.

SANDY: It's true.

KYLA: That is such a pile of crap. What fairy tale do you think this is? Prince Charming doesn't stay with Sleeping Beauty because he meets Snow White, who he leaves for Rapunzel, who he leaves for Goldilocks, who he leaves for Little Red Riding Hood. And note the theme here. Younger. Always younger.

SANDY: You're describing a certain number of men only.

KYLA: *Every* man is a seducible hound.

SANDY: That's not true.

KYLA: When push comes to shove and bump comes to grind, the trouser worm wins *every* time. No exceptions.

SANDY: That is absolutely not true.

KYLA: Name one. Including priests.

SANDY: Lou Gehrig.

KYLA: Based on?

SANDY: That movie.

KYLA: You mean *Pride of the Yankees*, the 1942 movie starring Gary Cooper and Teresa Wright? This is your evidence? A movie script? From the forties? That's a little feeble, isn't it? And P.S. Gary Cooper had a long, passionate affair with Patricia Neal while he was still married to his wife Veronica. No movies. They're all crap anyway. It's their fault we believe all this bogus, cotton candy, airy fairy—

SANDY: Charles Boyer. The real man.

KYLA: Based on?

SANDY: He committed suicide after his wife died.

KYLA: Which makes a good case for neediness, codependence, and emotional instability, but is hardly proof of fidelity. Get out of Hollywood. Look in the real world. How about people we actually know?

SANDY: Bobby Stratton.

KYLA: Oh yeah? Bobby? Of Bobby and Rebecca Cuddly-Pie?

SANDY: That's what I mean. I've never seen a couple more devoted to each other. He's always attentive, sends her flowers out of the blue, calls her from work—

KYLA: The man came on to me last New Year's Eve.

SANDY: At my house?

KYLA: In the bedroom when I went to get my coat. He came on so hard, I almost called "rape."

SANDY: You're kidding.

KYLA: I swear on my unfertilized eggs.

SANDY: Was he drunk?

KYLA: Does it matter?

SANDY: No. You're right. No.

KYLA: Yeah, the Cuddly-Pie has some curdled cream in it. It was disgusting. Kinda edges you over toward my little rancorous world, huh.

SANDY: All right. My grandfather. Married to my grandmother sixty-six years and has never strayed once in thought, word, or deed.

KYLA: How do you know?

SANDY: I just know. I know him.

KYLA: Yeah, you know him now, as a geezer. What about in his twenties or thirties?

SANDY: Not a chance.

KYLA: You don't know.

SANDY: He couldn't.

KYLA: How do you know?

SANDY: He isn't that kind of man.

KYLA: Sandy, *every* man is that kind of man. I'm telling you.

SANDY: All right. Richard.

KYLA: Well well well. I was wondering when you were going to mention St.

Richard the Wonderful. Kind of suspicious that you didn't lead with your own husband, if you're so sure and all.

SANDY: I don't want him inside this awful conversation.

KYLA: So you think St. Richard would never stray?

SANDY: Yes. Absolutely.

KYLA: You've got to be joking. I could seduce him in half an hour, and he doesn't even like me.

SANDY: He likes you all right.

KYLA: Fine, then make it fifteen minutes.

SANDY: You are high on bitterness.

KYLA: I'm telling you.

SANDY: It's impossible. I know Richard and I trust him completely.

KYLA: I could. Unmatched underwear and all.

SANDY: This is exactly why I didn't want to mention him, because I knew you'd turn it into some kind of dare or challenge or something. Think what you want. It would never happen.

KYLA: Wanna bet?

SANDY: No.

KYLA: So you have doubts.

SANDY: No, I have maturity.

KYLA: An excuse commonly used by the doubtful.

SANDY: I'm not making my husband or my marriage the subject of a mean-spirited bet.

KYLA: Look at it this way. If you're right, you're going to have the rare pleasure of seeing me make an ass of myself.

SANDY: I can see that in aerobics class.

KYLA: And well well well again. Someone is turning a little bitchy. Someone is maybe having a few doubts. Come on. Chicken? What have you got to lose?

SANDY: You as a friend.

KYLA: OK, so you won't take the bet. I'll consider that my proof.

SANDY: You can consider it anything you want. I know Richard and I'm not afraid of you.

KYLA: In fact, maybe I'll try anyway. Just to satisfy both our curiosities. Admit it. You are curious.

SANDY: Only about how you're going to feel when you lose.

KYLA: Ah, you'll probably tell him and ruin the sport.

SANDY: Why would I tell him? He'd say no on his own.

KYLA: You're that sure.

SANDY: Let me put it this way. If you can take him, you can have him.

KYLA: I can? Oh goody. And here I was going to settle for fifty bucks.

(Sandy lays money on the table for the bill.)

SANDY: And you know what you'd have? One less friend and one more cheating man on your list. I know you're hurting right now, so I'm not going to say what you deserve to hear, but be careful, Kyla. This is an ugly game you're playing.

(Sandy leaves.)

KYLA: All right. Then let the game begin.

(Lights down.)

END OF PLAY

The Giftbox

FRANCINE VOLPE

CHARACTERS
>A, a pregnant woman.
>C, her younger sister.

SETTING
>A kitchen in an upper-middle-class suburban home.

TIME
>The present.

NOTE: A slash (/) indicates that the next character begins to speak her line, overlapping the first speaker.

· · ·

C has just entered soaking wet and holding a large gift wrapped with a bow. A, visibly pregnant, faces her at the opposite end of the room.

A: My God you're all wet.

C: This is for you.

A: Look at you. You're all wet.

C: This is for—

A: Let me get you a towel you're all wet.

>*(A exits. C stares after her, still holding the box. A returns with a towel And without acknowledging the gift, deftly takes it from C, and pushes it aside on the counter.)*

A: *(Giving the towel.)* Here.

C: I'm sorry I missed the party.

>*(A cleans the counter.)*

A: The shower?

C: I was at the doctor.

A: People get sick you can't do anything about it.

C: I got you something.

A: You shouldn't have done that.

C: It's nothing big.

A: But you didn't have to.

C: But I did.

>*(As she speaks C takes the gift and puts it on a table centerstage. A watches.)*

C: I bought a gift box and everything.

A: You didn't have to spend a lot of money.

C: I didn't.

A: Have you talked to Mom?

C: You mean today?

A: No . . . just in general.

(C approaches the counter and takes an apple from a basket as if she owns the place.)

C: Can I have this?

A: . . . Sure.

(C eats the apple with no knife, no plate, no napkin. A watches her getting it all over.)

C: *(With her mouth full.)* Do you have a napkin? Mom's pissed I missed your party.

A: If you were sick you were sick.

C: I was at the doctor.

A: Nothing you can do.

C: I brought you a gift. Don't you want to open it?

A: . . . I'd rather wait for Nicky,

C: You open all your other presents at the party . . . And like . . . sit in a fancy rented wicker chair?

A: Nicky was there.

C: You really pussy-whipped him into sitting there, huh?

A: It's customary now.

C: Did he wear a hat decorated with ribbons and wrapping paper?

A: That's for a wedding shower.

C: Did he like hold up like the pots so everyone could see them?

A: You can look at the registry if you want.

C: But you ate tea sandwiches, right?

A: Nicky's mother ordered traditional Greek food.

C: Did you tell her we were Jews?

A: No.

(C doesn't know what to do with the apple core. A watches her put it on the counter.)

C: Does he have friends?

A: Excuse me?

C: Does Nick have his own friends?

A: I don't think I understand the question.

A: Like who are Nick's friends?

A: Why don't you ask him?

C: I wish I were marrying Nick.

A: Since when is he your type?

C: And get presents.

A: The presents are for the baby.

C: But you are going to marry Nick, aren't you?

A: Not for the presents I'm not.

C: Then for why?

A: Because I want to get married.

C: Me too I want to get married too.

A: You could have fooled me.

C: . . . You don't think I'm marriage material.

A: Do you?

C: I don't know, why don't you tell me what's wrong with me?

A: I don't think anything's wrong with you.

C: Yes you do.

A: No I don't.

C: Yes you do.

A: No I don't.

C: Yes you do.

A: No I don't.

    (Silence.)

C: . . . Yes you—

A: That shirt.

C: What?

A: That shirt.

C: What shirt?

A: Don't ever wear it again.

C: This shirt?

A: Don't wear it again as long as you live, you want to get married.

C: . . . This?

A: You look like Joan Jett.

C: You think I look like a lesbian?

A: You look like a teenaged prostitute.

C: How scary is that. White-collar men troll around looking for them in their
    SUVs. Are you scared?

A: No.

C: Nobody loves me and it's because of this shirt.

A: You're sending a message.

C: I hate this fucking shirt . . . You know. Turn of the century. Nobody'd marry a woman if she was seen unescorted. Or in the 1920s if she smoked cigarettes. Midcentury. If she got pregnant out of wedlock. Like you.

A: How does this relate to what I'm saying?

C: The reason you were able to get finger-fucked in the seventh grade without getting your teeth knocked out with a brick is because women like me stayed single. Ruminate on that.

A: Once again. How does this relate to what I'm saying?

C: I change this shirt, progress comes to a blinding halt.

A: Then keep wearing it.

(C smiles mischievously at A. A strange pause.)

C: You have to admit that you're dying to know what's in that box.

(Silently, they look at the gift box.)

A: I wish you didn't spend any of your money.

C: I know especially since Mom paid my last Visa bill, I have no business buying anyone any gifts.

A: I only mean that I have everything I need.

C: Do you?

A: I think so, yes.

C: You sure?

A: Why don't you just tell me what it is?

C: It's a bomb and it's going to go off in five more minutes.

A: You shouldn't say things like that.

C: That's right, you're precious—I mean pregnant.

A: Do you want to leave?

C: *(Sincere now.)* . . . No.

A: Then what do you want?

C: I want to say. First . . . I'm really really really really sorry that I couldn't make it to your party.

A: You were sick.

C: I was at the doctor.

A: That couldn't be helped.

C: And I need money.

(A stares at her. C looks back at her. Silence.)

A: No.

C: . . . Oh.

A: You have learn to be more responsible with money.

C: Actually no. No I don't. I don't have to do anything.

(In an instant this spirals into the inevitable, the same old yelling over one another, the same fight they've been having for twenty years.)

A: NO. You're wrong. You do. You do have to learn how / to

C: You've never paid a bill with your own money in your whole / life

A: You have to learn to respect me. In my house. In my / house

C: Have you ever respected me?

A: I swore I swore I swore I was not going to let you get to me / this time.

C: When have you ever respected me?

A: I swore I wasn't going to do it can't believe it I can't believe I let you get to me / you—

C: Oh just shut up and give me the money.

(A has had it.)

A: Respect yourself you fucking brat.

C: I do respect / myself

A: Oh, grow up. You go from temp job to temp job with that dumb haircut.

C: I have taught literacy in third world countries.

A: Oh save it, you're like poison.

C: I have helped impoverished—

A: Shut up.

(Pause.)

C: That you know nothing about.

A: On whose dime? Mom's? So Mom has to work at sixty-seven years old so you could scribble poems with a bunch of seven-year-old girls in Laos?

(C is starting to get upset.)

C: . . . What I do is important.

A: Then how come you don't have any money?

C: *(She sincerely tears up.)* Because I don't have a husband. *(C cries from a real place.)* Oh . . . Oh . . . Oh. I'm . . . I'm . . . I'm so lonely. I'm sorry I'm. I'm just so . . . I'm so sorry. I'm so lonely. Oh God I . . . Oh.

(A is taken aback. C, shaken, walks to the table with the gift box to rest. She cries. A watches her. Feels bad. A approaches. C moves the gift box to the side.)

C: I'm sorry. You're right. You don't need this. I'm sorry.

(A exits. C sits alone. A returns with a checkbook and pen. She sits at the table.)

A: How much do you need.

(C looks at her. A writes out a check. She slides the check to C, who looks at it. They face each other.)

A: Just let me say one thing. I was an artist. You know that I was an artist. I wanted to act. You know that I studied. I went to that scene study class. I had a vocal coach. You know I had that coach. I wanted it. But I couldn't get a break. Nobody wanted to see me. Did you know I was about to get signed? Big agency. About to sign me. Big big agency. Big agency. Just when I found out I was pregnant. I didn't know how I felt about it all. No really. But. So I went to the movies. I went and saw a movie. And in the movie there was a family. That made all the wrong choices. And their bad choices led to misery. Just . . . misery. And in the end they commit suicide. They tie bags over their heads. And we see their distorted faces like masks.

I don't ever have to act. Not ever again. To . . . For what? To participate in that? To participate in that. So that everyone can sit and watch the people die. Watching them living and dying . . . at the same time.

I just. Felt what was important. And then it was clear. What was important was clear to me. I hope that you have that moment. I do. I don't want you to be so confused. I don't. And I love you. And I know. In the end. All this acting out. All this. It's because that's really all you want to hear from me.

(Silence.)

C: Are you fucking kidding me?

A: Get out.

(C crumples check.)

C: You wanna know what I want to hear from you? You wanna know what I want to hear? "Why were you at the doctor."

A: Good. Good. Fine. Why were you at the doctor?

C: Why don't you ask Nick. Because he was not at your party opening gifts. He was with me.

(C gets up to leave. A pushes C, stopping her from exiting.)

A: You're a liar.

C: You're a liar. Did you know he had two abortions? Did you know that? He told me. He got two other girls pregnant before you. That he knew of. He told me.

A: You're making me sick.

C: And YOU ARE MAKING ME SICK. I didn't sleep with your boyfriend. OK he's my friend, he's my friend. And you are not my friend. I had to ask a stranger to drive me to a clinic and I couldn't call you because I knew what I'd get from you. I know you. You see I know you. You'd rather make yourself feel righteous then help me. Then help me. Then help. You want to know why you can't act? Because you're not capable of ever imagining yourself as someone else. You act like good fortune is some kind of reward for good behavior, but the world doesn't work like that. The world is inexplicable, I know it. I know it because I've seen it.

But you never asked me. You never asked me where I was going. Or where I'd been. Or what I'd seen. You cut yourself off. You've cut yourself off from it . . . But the world . . . the world is vast. And it is filled with all the people you will never see. And all that you will never be . . . So how many abortions have you had? Think. How many abortions have you had? *(Slides the wrapped gift box to her, and like a roar.)* I dare you. I dare you. I dare you to look inside that box.

(C exits. A, shaken, collects herself. Regards the gift box for a while as the lights dim around the box. She takes a step toward it. And another. She confronts it. She takes a deep, deep breath in. Blackout.)

END OF PLAY

Hollywood Hills

STEPHANIE ALISON WALKER

First produced by Moving Arts at the Steve Allen Theatre,
Los Angeles, July 2007, as part of the The Car Plays.
Directed by Paul Nicolai Stein. Cast: D—Kathi Chandler;
Missy—Jenifer Kingsley.

CHARACTERS

> MISSY, twenty-two years old. A Hollywood starlet in the making. Recreational coke user, occasional eater, fanatical exerciser.
>
> D, twenty-four years old. Considers herself the older and wiser of the two friends. D works as a stand-in.

SETTING

> A giant SUV, somewhere in the Hollywood Hills.

TIME

> The present: 2 AM.

• • •

At rise: Lights up as Missy, in the driver's seat, finishes snorting a line of coke. D, in the passenger seat, watches her. Both girls are dressed in skimpy Hollywood clubbing clothes.

D: You have no idea how to get there, do you?
   (D goes to light a cigarette.)
MISSY: What do you think you're doing?! You can't smoke up here!
D: Shut up.
MISSY: No, serious. There are signs all over. There's no smoking in the Hollywood Hills.
D: Are your ears ringing? My ears are totally ringing.
MISSY: Listen to me!
D: You are like the loudest person I've ever met.
   (She goes once again to light the smoke.)
MISSY: Don't!
   (D stops.)
MISSY: I'm serious. You'll, like, start a fire or something. It's really really dry. You could start a fire, and it would spread so fast the whole city would burn down or something.
D: You don't know what you're talking about. And you don't know where we're going. We're lost and you're high and I'm not listening to you.
MISSY: You're the navigator. It's your fault we're lost.
   (D throws an ink-smeared cocktail napkin at Missy.)
D: See if you can read it.
MISSY: It's all smeared.

D: You think?

MISSY: Why's it all smeared? It wasn't like that when I handed it to you.

D: Yes it was.

MISSY: No, I remember—

D: You're high.

MISSY: I'm focused. *(Beat.)* I remember him saying it was just south of Mulholland. Or something.

D: South of Mulholland or something?

MISSY: Yes. OK?

D: That could be anywhere.

(D goes to light the cigarette again. Missy grabs the cigarette from D's lips and throws it.)

D: Hey!

MISSY: I'm serious! No smoking! You're really freaking me out, and I don't need that right now. I'm already totally freaked out about running into Mark with that stupid One Tree Hill ho-bag.

D: Everything is always about you.

MISSY: Serious. Do you really need a cigarette that bad that you can't wait until we get to the party?

D: If we ever find it.

MISSY: We'll find it! We must have missed the turn. We'll go back.

D: We're not gonna find it. We're totally lost. Let's just go home.

MISSY: No. We're going to the party. Do you know who's gonna be there?!

D: Mark?

MISSY: That's not who I meant.

D: The only reason you want to go is to spy on Mark.

MISSY: No. That's not why.

D: Then why?

MISSY: Because. Lots of reasons. I want to see the house. I heard it's amazing. Some famous architect designed it or something.

D: Really? Who?

MISSY: I don't know. Someone famous.

D: It's already two AM, Missy.

MISSY: So?! Adam Brody will be there. He seemed totally into you at the club. I could put in a good word.

D: Doesn't he have a girlfriend?

MISSY: I don't know. Does it matter? You look hot tonight.

D: Take me home, take me home, take me home.

MISSY: You can't just turn down an invitation from someone like that, D. Word will get out that you're antisocial. And that'll be the end of your career.

D: I have to get up early tomorrow . . . for my career.

MISSY: For what?

D: I told you like twenty times!

MISSY: No you didn't. I don't remember.

D: The Hilary Duff movie!?!

(Missy shakes her head, not remembering.)

D: I told you at least ten times. I'm her stand-in. I have to be on set at seven A.M. That's in, like, five hours.

MISSY: You don't even look like her.

D: I don't have to look like her, I just have to be the same size. You don't listen to anything I say, ever, do you? Just take me home. I need to get a good night's sleep.

MISSY: What is wrong with you?!

D: I'm tired. We're lost. You won't let me smoke.

MISSY: You know, you might actually have fun at the party.

(Missy looks at herself in the mirror. She rubs some coke on her teeth. Then runs her tongue over her teeth.)

D: I gotta pee.

(D opens the door to get out.)

MISSY: Where are you going?!

D: To pee. I just said that.

MISSY: Out there?!

D: You want me to pee in here?

MISSY: No! Gross! Can't you hold it?

D: I've been holding it since we left the club because you wouldn't let me go there.

MISSY: Because only losers wait in line!

D: My bladder's about to burst.

MISSY: What about coyotes?!

D: You're such a prissy bitch.

MISSY: Or snakes.

D: I'll take my chances.

(D gets out of the car and exits.)

MISSY: Or serial killers!

(Missy looks at herself in the mirror. She primps. Obsessively. After a few beats, D returns and something in the headlights grabs her attention. She looks into the headlights, stricken. Missy is suddenly startled by D's presence and screams

a short, sharp scream. She then lays on the horn and sticks her head out the window.)

MISSY: Let's go!

(D walks slowly around to the passenger side and silently gets back in. Missy continues her obsessive primping in her coke-induced frenzy.)

MISSY: I am pretty, right? I mean, I'm not fishing for complements, I just want to confirm that my perspective is accurate. That I'm pretty, because I'm pretty sure I am. I'm hot, right? I am. I mean, I'm a size two, I've got a perfectly symmetrical face and great tits. Mark always talked about my tits. And they're real! Not like that stupid bimbo's. What's her name, anyway? Cherry? Cherish? You know, just because you book a guest spot on One Tree Hill doesn't make you a star. I hate that attitude. I mean, how many people actually watch that show anyway? And did you see her? She was all like expecting everyone at the club to recognize her. So sad. Drinking Red Bull vodka as if that were still cool. It's sad. Someone should really tell her. I have no idea how Mark could be into her. And she can't act. She's horrible! I can't even look at her she's so fucking embarrassingly bad. How the fuck did she get that part?! It's not like she's hot. She's all soft and puffy and . . . round. *(Crying.)* What does Mark see in her?!

D: Shut up.

MISSY: What the fuck is wrong with you?! I'm in agony here and all you can say is "shut up"?!

D: We should've taken a cab.

MISSY: I told you I'd find it! I just need to find my *Thomas Guide.* It's in here somewhere.

D: You're in no condition to drive.

MISSY: Oh, and you are?!

D: No! That's why I said we should've taken a cab. Because if we had taken a cab, we wouldn't have gotten lost and you wouldn't have been driving and there wouldn't be a goddamned person stuck to the grate of your fucking SUV!

(A long beat.)

MISSY: Um . . . what, what did you say?

D: We should've taken a cab.

MISSY: Not that part.

D: Remember when there was that, like, thump or thud and we thought we hit a speed bump—which seemed weird because why would there be just one speed bump all the way out here?

MISSY: What are you talking about?

D: It wasn't a speed bump.

MISSY: What wasn't a speed bump?

D: The thud! There was a thud and I said, "What was that?!" And you said, "A speed bump." And I said, "That's weird."

MISSY: Yeah?

D: It wasn't a speed bump.

MISSY: What was it?

D: *(Big sigh.)* It was a person, Missy.

MISSY: You're such a bitch. I don't know why I'm friends with you.

D: Shut. Up!

MISSY: That's not funny. This isn't funny, D.

D: I know! I know! I know!

MISSY: Wait, wait wait. Please tell me you're joking. *(Beat.)* Tell me you're—

D: I'm not joking!

MISSY: You're fucking with me. You're trying to freak me out just so I'll take you home so you don't have to go to the party with me.

D: Go look.

MISSY: What?

D: See for yourself.

MISSY: It's dark out. Maybe you didn't see right. It could be something else. A skunk. A possum.

D: A person.

MISSY: A coyote.

D: A human.

MISSY: No! It could be a cat.

D: It's not a cat.

MISSY: Or a dog. I hope not. But it could be. It happens.

D: You hit someone with your car and they're stuck there. Right now. Like dying or dead. I can't tell. But there's blood. A LOT of blood. Blood and, like, guts and stuff. It's really, really gross. It's like CSI gross.

MISSY: OK, then. Who is it? Where did they come from?

D: I don't know! How would I know? I was looking for street signs. You were supposed to be focusing on the road.

MISSY: I was. And I didn't see anyone.

D: Just because you didn't see anyone doesn't mean they're not there, Missy.

MISSY: This is the worst joke anyone has ever played in the entire history of the world and you are the worst friend ever. Ever! You can totally forget about me putting in a good word for you with Adam Brody!

D: We need to call an ambulance.

MISSY: Are you serious?

D: If they're not dead already, they will be soon.

MISSY: You know, just because you did one episode of *ER* doesn't make you a
    fucking doctor, OK?

D: Do you really want to let them die?!

MISSY: Let who die?

D: Get out of the fucking car and look! NOW!

    (A beat.)

MISSY: Fine. Jeez.

    *(Missy unbuckles her seatbelt, opens the door, and climbs out. Missy slowly
    walks around to the front of the car. She looks down. A beat. Another beat.
    Nothing registers on her face. She suddenly leans over and vomits. D pulls a
    cigarette out of the pack and goes to light it. It doesn't light. The lighter is
    out of fluid. She tries a few times. Missy finishes vomiting and gets back in
    the car. She does a line of coke. D tries the lighter again. It works. She looks
    at the flame. Missy looks at D and holds her in her gaze for a beat.)*

MISSY: Don't even think about lighting that mother-fucking cigarette!

    (D looks at MISSY, lights the cigarette, opens the door, and gets out.)

MISSY: D!

    (D slams the door shut and walks away.)

MISSY: D?

    (Missy slides down in her seat. Lights fade out.)

END OF PLAY

RIGHTS AND PERMISSIONS